Developing Family and Community Involvement Skills Through Case Studies and Field Experiences

Ronald E. Diss
Emory & Henry College

Pamela K. Buckley
The Gallup Organization

PEARSON

Merrill
Prentice Hall

Upper Saddle River, New Jersey
Columbus, Ohio

Library of Congress Cataloging-in-Publication Data

Diss, Ronald E.
    Developing family and community involvement skills through case studies and field
experiences / Ronald E. Diss, Pamela K. Buckley.
        p. cm.
Includes bibliographical references and index.
    ISBN 0-13-048622-1
    1. Education—Parent participation—United States—Case studies. 2. Education—Parent particpation—
United States—Field work. 3. Community and school—United States—Case studies. 4. Community and
school—United States—Field work. I. Buckley, Pamela K. II. Title.

LB1048.5.D57 2005
371.19'2—dc22   2003025658

Vice President and Executive Publisher: Jeffery W. Johnston
Publisher: Kevin M. Davis
Development Editor: Julie Peters
Editorial Assistant: Autumn Benson
Production Editor: Sheryl Glicker Langner
Design Coordinator: Diane C. Lorenzo
Photo Coordinator: Valerie Schultz
Cover Design: Ali Mohrman
Cover Image: Index Stock
Production Manager: Laura Messerly
Director of Marketing: Ann Castel Davis
Marketing Manager: Autumn Purdy
Marketing Coordinator: Tyra Poole

This book was set in Optima by Carlisle Communications, Ltd. It was printed and bound by R. R. Donnelley &
Sons Company. The cover was printed by The Lehigh Press, Inc.

Photo Credits: Scott Cunningham/Merrill, pp. 10, 28, 48, 118; Jeff Greenberg/PhotoEdit, p. 13; Barnabas
Kindersley/Dorling Kindersley Media Library, p. 15; Tim Cairns/Merrill, p. 24; Todd Yarrington/Merrill, pp. 26,
103; Anne Vega/Merrill, pp. 30, 42, 62, 96; Lynn Saville/Prentice Hall School Division, p. 32; Eugene Gordon/
PH College, p. 44; Laima Drukis/PH College, pp. 45, 46; Michal Heron/PH College, pp. 56, 76; CEM/Merrill,
p. 58; Zane Williams/Getty Images, Inc.–Store Allstock, p. 65; Anthony Magnacca/Merrill, pp. 67, 79, 104, 107,
122, 125, 131; Ken Karp/PH College, p. 84; Shirley Zeiberg/PH College, pp. 86, 134; Tom Watson/Merrill, p. 99;
Kathy Kirtland/Merrill, p. 129.

Pearson Prentice Hall™ is a trademark of Pearson Education, Inc.
Pearson® is a registered trademark of Pearson plc
Prentice Hall® is a registered trademark of Pearson Education, Inc.
Merrill® is a registered trademark of Pearson Education, Inc.

Pearson Education Ltd.
Pearson Education Singapore Pte. Ltd.
Pearson Education Canada, Ltd.
Pearson Education–Japan

Pearson Education Australia Pty. Limited
Pearson Education North Asia Ltd.
Pearson Educación de Mexico, S.A. de C.V.
Pearson Education Malaysia Pte. Ltd.

10 9 8 7 6 5 4 3 2
ISBN: 0-13-048622-1

We dedicate this book to all people everywhere who strive to nurture the lives of others, and to our children: John Diss, Lily Diss Westcott, Christopher Westcott, DeeAnn Buckley, Patrick Buckley, and Michael and Susan Carter Buckley.

Acknowledgments

In writing this book we have drawn upon our more than 30 years of experience in various contexts with many people. In our lives as students, teachers, colleagues, and family members, we have acquired a rich legacy. We count among these rich experiences the insights we have gained about teaching, learning, and family and community involvement. The countless people with whom we have learned, worked, and lived have taught us what we know, and inspired us to write this book. We acknowledge their contributions with much gratitude. Over the course of our professional lives we have been fortunate to have interacted with many outstanding teachers, students, and families. We have worked with teachers who achieved teaching excellence under a variety of challenging circumstances. We have also witnessed the joys and struggles of families representing various structures, socioeconomic levels, and educational backgrounds in their efforts to provide the best for their children. More often than not, we have experienced teachers and family members who want to work together as partners to provide the best possible education for their children. We especially want to acknowledge the insights we have gained from these teachers and families.

We are grateful to Gerald Clay and Ethyl Haughton, professors of education at Bluefield College, Virginia, for pilot testing the case studies with their teacher education students.

We would also like to acknowledge the reviewers of this book whose insights and suggestions were invaluable to the quality and completion of this project. They include Rachel Adeodu, Northeastern Illinois University; Jaesook Gilbert, Eastern Kentucky University; Charles B. Hennon, Miami University; Nancy A. Howard, Bellarmine University; Candace Kaye, California State University, Long Beach; Marion O'Brien, University of North Carolina at Greensboro; Jana Sanders, Texas A&M University, Corpus Christi; and Alan C. Taylor, Syracuse University.

Additionally, we want to thank the professional staff at Merrill/Prentice Hall, whose skills, direction, and encouragement were invaluable in bringing this book to fruition. Last, but not least, we wish to thank John Buckley who, over many months, gave of his time and talent to assist the authors whenever needed.

About the Authors

Ronald Diss is director of educational outreach and professor of education at Emory & Henry College in Virginia. **Pamela Buckley** is director of marketing for the Government Division of The Gallup Organization in Washington, DC. They have coauthored a number of articles on teacher education and presented papers at national teacher education association conferences on teacher effectiveness, parent involvement, and rural education.

Ron Diss received his Ed.D. from Virginia Polytechnic Institute and State University. He has taught elementary, middle, and high school grades in private and public schools, where he also was an elementary school principal. At Emory & Henry College he teaches undergraduate and graduate courses in child development and reading education. He has also supervised student teachers and directed the college's Mentor Teacher Preparation Program, the Early Field Experience Program, and the Office of Academic Support Services. Diss is active in providing professional development to improve literacy education in K–12 schools. In addition to several articles on reflective practice, he is the author of *Recruiting and Training Volunteer Tutors for Emergent and Beginning Readers,* and a companion training video titled *The ABC's of Tutoring* to assist parents, teachers, and community volunteers working with children in need of support to develop literacy skills. Diss is a past president of the Association of Teacher Educators in Virginia, and a sitting member of Virginia's Advisory Board on Teacher Education and Licensure (ABTEL).

Pam Buckley received her Ed. D. from the University of Houston. She has taught remedial and developmental reading, English, and social studies in junior and senior high schools, adult basic education courses in a community college, and teacher education courses at the university level. While completing her doctoral work at the University of Houston, Buckley directed the Houston Area Teacher Center, supervised student teachers, and taught undergraduate courses in classroom management. She was director of the Commonwealth Center for the Education of Teachers at James Madison University, where she encouraged and supported innovative practices in teacher education among Virginia's 37 public and private teacher preparation institutions. Buckley is a former vice president of Appalachia Educational Laboratory, where she also directed the Appalachia Eisenhower Regional Math/Science Consortium and the Region IV Comprehensive Technical Assistance Center. She has published articles on teacher education in *Science Educator, Issues & Inquiry in College Learning and Teaching,* and the *Journal of Staff*

Development. In addition to her work in education, she has had wide experience working in business and private industry in the United States and the Middle East.

Diss and Buckley have written this book to inspire and enable educators to reach out to families and community agencies to establish meaningful partnerships.

Educator Learning Center: An Invaluable Online Resource

Merrill Education and the Association for Supervision and Curriculum Development (ASCD) invite you to take advantage of a new online resource, one that provides access to the top research and proven strategies associated with ASCD and Merrill—the Educator Learning Center. At **www.EducatorLearningCenter.com** you will find resources that will enhance your students, understanding of course topics and of current educational issues, in addition to being invaluable for further research.

HOW THE EDUCATOR LEARNING CENTER WILL HELP YOUR STUDENTS BECOME BETTER TEACHERS

With the combined resources of Merrill Education and ASCD, you and your students will find a wealth of tools and materials to better prepare them for the classroom.

Research

- More than 600 articles from the ASCD journal *Educational Leadership* discuss everday issues faced by practicing teachers.
- A direct link on the site to Research Navigator™ gives students access to many of the leading education journals, as well as extensive content detailing the research process.
- Excerpts from Merrill Education texts give your students insights on important topics of instructional methods, diverse populations, assessment, classroom management, technology, and refining classroom practice.

Classroom Practice

- Hundreds of lesson plans and teaching strategies are categorized by content area and age range.
- Case studies and classroom video footage provide virtual field experience for student reflection.
- Computer simulations and other electronic tools keep your students abreast of today's classrooms and current technologies.

LOOK INTO THE VALUE OF EDUCATOR LEARNING CENTER YOURSELF

A four-month subscription to Educator Learning Center is $25 but is **FREE** when used in conjunction with this text. To obtain free passcodes for your students, simply contact your Merrill/Prentice Hall sales representative, and your representative will give you a special ISBN to give your bookstore when ordering your textbooks. To preview the value of this website to you and your students, please go to **www.EducatorLearningCenter.com** and click on "Demo."

Discover the Companion Website Accompanying This Book

THE PRENTICE HALL COMPANION WEBSITE: A VIRTUAL LEARNING ENVIRONMENT

Technology is a constantly growing and changing aspect of our field that is creating a need for content and resources. To address this emerging need, Prentice Hall has developed an online learning envrionment for students and professors alike—Companion Websites—to support our textbooks.

In creating a Companion Website, our goal is to build on and enhance what the textbook already offers. For this reason, the content for each user-friendly website is organized by topic and provides the professor and student with a variety of meaningful resources. Common features of a Companion Website include:

FOR THE PROFESSOR—

Every Companion Website integrates **Syllabus Manager™,** an online syllabus creation and management utility.

- **Syllabus Manager™** provides you, the instructor, with an easy, step-by-step process to create and revise syllabi, with direct links into Companion Website and other online content without having to learn HTML.
- Students may logon to your syllabus during any study session. All they need to know is the web address for the Companion Website and the password you've assigned to your syllabus.
- After you have created a syllabus using **Syllabus Manager™,** students may enter the syllabus for their course section from any point in the Companion Website.
- Clicking on a date, the student is shown the list of activities for the assignment. The activities for each assignment are linked directly to actual content, saving time for students.
- Adding assignments consists of clicking on the desired due date, then filling in the details of the assignments—name of the assignment, instructions, and whether or not it is a one-time or repeating assignment.
- In addition, links to other activites can be created easily. If the activity is online, a URL can be entered in the space provided, and it will be linked automatically in the final syllabus.
- Your completed syllabus is hosted on our servers, allowing convenient updates from any computer on the Internet. Changes you make to your syllabus are immediately available to your students at their next logon.

FOR THE STUDENT—

- *Introduction*—General information about the topic and how it will be covered in the website.
- *Web Links*—A variety of websites related to topic areas.
- *Timely Articles*—Links to online articles that enable you to become more aware of important issues in early childhood.
- *Learn by Doing*—Put concepts into action, participate in activities, examine strategies, and more.
- *Visit a School*—Visit a school's website to see concepts, theories, and strategies in action.

- *For Teachers/Practitioners*—Access information you will need to know as an educator including information on materials, activites, and lessons.
- *Current Policies and Standards*—Find out the latest early childhood policies from the government and various organizations, and view state, federal, and curriculum standards.
- *Resources and Organizations*—Discover tools to help you plan your classroom or center and organizations to provide current information and standards for each topic.
- *Electronic Bluebook*—Paperless method of completing homework or essays assigned by a professor. Finished work can be sent to the professor via email.
- *Message Board*—Virtual bulletin board to post and respond to questions and comments from a national audience.

To take advantage of these and other resources, please visit the *Developing Family and Community Involvement Skills Through Case Studies and Field Experiences* Companion Website at

www.prenhall.com/diss

Brief Contents

Contents

Chapter 3   Understanding Families of Varying Income Levels   42

Chapter 6   *Understanding Families of Children with Special Needs*   *96*

Note: Every effort has been made to provide accurate and current Internet information in this book. However, the Internet and information posted on it are constantly changing, and it is inevitable that some of the Internet addresses listed in this textbook will change.

INTRODUCTION

Family involvement is one of the more important issues affecting American education today. Research confirms that partnerships between schools and families* result in better school attendance, fewer dropouts, decreased delinquency, and improved student achievement (Henderson & Berla, 1994; U.S. Department of Education, 1994). Although everyone acknowledges that family involvement should be a priority, effective comprehensive school–community partnerships are rare.

Traditionally, school activities designed to involve families have included back-to-school nights, PTA or PTO meetings, parent conferences, and fundraising. Although these activities provide opportunities for families to visit the school, the scope of involvement is limited. Families that make an effort to attend often find themselves in the role of passive listeners, not active partners.

Unfortunately, administrators and teachers commonly lack the skills to initiate and nurture family participation in schooling (Farkas, Johnson, & Duffett, 1999; Kendall, 1993). In fact, recent survey results released by the National PTA indicate that no state requires a course in parent involvement for teacher licensure. Only a few states include parent involvement in competency requirements and training program standards for teachers and administrators. In addition, no state requires parent involvement coursework for renewal of a teaching license (National PTA, 1998).

When effective home–school partnerships are not established, student achievement suffers and teachers experience increased frustration and professional disappointment. Although both of these outcomes are common, they could be greatly reduced if teachers were better prepared to involve families in children's schooling.

*Throughout this book all references to "parent" or "family" may be interpreted broadly to include any and all adults who play an important role in a child's family life.

3

We have written this book primarily to help preservice teachers and school personnel (e.g., teachers, administrators, and counselors) develop the necessary skills to involve families and communities as partners in K–12 education.

The book is also appropriate for adding a service-learning component to a variety of professional studies courses and to service providers other than educators who need to learn about family involvement. A survey of training programs in eight related fields conducted by the Carolina Institute for Research on Infant Personnel Preparation found that programs in nutrition, psychology, special education, and speech–language pathology all needed additional course content in family involvement (Bailey, Simeonsson, Yoder, & Huntington, 1990). This list reasonably could be extended to include occupational and physical therapists and members of the social service professions. Winton and DiVenere (1995) suggest that most professionals in early intervention have received little training on how to collaborate with families. For this reason, references to teachers in this text include the broader professional audience.

Each chapter addresses a significant characteristic of the contemporary family followed by an **Application** section and a **Supplemental Activities** section designed to teach the dynamics of effective home–school partnerships. The **Application** section includes practical **strategies** for working with those families characterized in the chapter and a **case study** and **discussion guide** related to the chapter's content. The **Supplemental Activities** section includes **school-based** and **community-based field experiences, response journal prompts,** and **role playing** and **reflection exercises.** The strategies, case studies, field experiences, and other activities are designed to encourage students to examine, reflect, and construct meaning about family structures, attitudes toward family involvement, the complexities associated with establishing effective home–school partnerships, and to learn about social service agencies that provide family support and resources.

The themes in the text address the significant areas of change that are characteristic of the contemporary American family. Each chapter provides an overview of the key issues, rather than an in-depth treatment because the text is intended to complement the content of professional studies courses by adding a family involvement component without overburdening existing course curricula. These themes are developed in other sources in greater depth for those who desire more extensive information.

Chapter 1 describes significant areas of change in the structure of contemporary American families, ethnic and cultural demographics, income levels, and families with children who have special needs. The case study at the end of Chapter 1, "Who's Responsible for Damien?", presents a situation in which a teacher and a single parent have difficulty communicating because of differing expectations for each other's roles and responsibilities. Chapter 2 focuses on the family's role in education and the impact of family involvement. The case study at the end of Chapter 2, "Can't Rules be Bent?", highlights how a single father's experience with poor school-to-home communication and an unbending school policy make it almost impossible for him to form any type of meaningful partnership with his son's school. Chapter 3 describes challenges to viable home–school partnerships with families of varying income levels. The case study at the end of Chapter 3, "Is Anyone Listening?", presents a young girl who feels isolated and different from her classmates because of her family's lower socioeconomic status. She is a target of ridicule from her peers because of her physical appearance and lack of resources. Chapter 4 addresses how families from different cultures view their roles in their children's education. The case study at the end of Chapter 4, "Who Suffers When Cultures Collide?", highlights the situation of a young Asian American girl who runs into difficulty when others are insensitive to her culture. Chapter 5 describes nontraditional families and different parenting styles. The case study at the end of Chapter 5, "How Do Family Structures Affect Classroom Instruction?", illustrates a situation in which a teacher unwittingly isolates a student from his peers and focuses negative attention on the young man because he doesn't consider different family structures when making an assignment. Chapter 6 discusses families of children who have special needs including those who are gifted and talented. The case study at the end of Chapter 6, "Who's Responsible When a Child with Special Needs Fails?", describes a gifted and talented student who also has special learning needs. Chapter 7 presents four profiles of schools that have involved families in effective home–school partnerships. The case study at the end of Chapter 7, "Developing a Plan," suggests strategies for schools to establish successful school–home partnerships.

LEARNING WITH CASE STUDIES

Cases are a highly effective way of helping learners understand complex issues (Ball, Lambert, & Rosenberg, 1991; Doyle, 1990; Feltovich, Spiro, & Coulson, 1997; Merseth, 1996; Wasserman, 1994). The cases are meant to stimulate reflection and discussion about the complexities of classrooms and family involvement. As learners discuss the cases, they identify interrelated features and uncover the many layers of issues surrounding critical aspects of the cases. Discussing and analyzing cases helps developing teachers gain valuable experience understanding issues and forming realistic solutions to complex problems related to family involvement. Although short, the cases contain multiple strands of inquiry into critical issues affecting home–school partnerships. The cases can be used in a variety of program structures (e.g., classrooms, seminars, or workshops), and may be taught within a 1-hour time frame or longer. Specific suggestions on how to teach with cases are given in Appendix B.

LEARNING DURING FIELD EXPERIENCES AND REFLECTIVE EXERCISES

Field experiences offer opportunities for preservice teachers to learn the dynamics of effective home–school partnerships through *inquiry, observation and participation,* and *dialogue,* a process practiced by effective teachers to inform their teaching decisions (Borko & Putnam, 2000; Greeno & the Middle School through Applications Project Group, 1998; Wildman & Niles, 1987). Research indicates that experience in this reflective process enables preservice teachers to learn the skills they will need to be successful practitioners in classrooms characterized by increasingly complex contexts (Diss & Kolenbrander, 1993; Kersh, 1995).

To be effective, teachers must continuously reflect on their teaching decisions and modify their practices to enhance student achievement. Early field experiences provide an excellent context for introducing preservice teachers to this critically necessary reflective process.

It has been well established that classrooms are highly complex social environments (Brophy, 1988; Brophy & Good, 1986; Kersh, 1995; Schon, 1983). These environments are characterized by ever-changing contexts that teachers must constantly monitor to make appropriate instructional decisions (Borko & Putnam, 1996). Successful teachers know about these phenomena and use reflection and other technical skills to organize and deliver instruction accordingly (Cazden, 1981; Feltovich et al., 1997; Gold, 1996; Posner, 1995; Putnam, 1984). Understandably, learning these skills is viewed as an ongoing process (Greeno, 1997; McNamara, 1995; Wildman & Niles, 1987), and educators are best served when they are introduced to this process early in their teacher preparation experience (Greeno & the Middle School through Applications Project Group, 1998; Guy, 1993; Shulman, 1987; Wildman & Niles, 1987).

As Kersh (1995) reminds us,

> Knowing why a plan, an activity, or a total curriculum is a success (or failure) is as important as knowing it was successful. Knowing the rationale, the context, and the theory of successful learning experiences requires reflection on that experience. Student teachers should understand they will learn not from experience but from reflection on that experience. Preparation programs must demand reflection on practice so frequently that it becomes a habit of teaching. (p. 103)

Teachers need to learn early in their teacher preparation programs strategies for involving families in the education of their children (Evans-Schilling, 1996; Harvard Family Research Project, 1997). Teacher educators and program directors can help future teachers develop these skills by designing early field experiences that include inquiry about school and classroom events, observation and participation in schools, dialogue (with peers, school personnel, and professors), and reflection on their observations of what school personnel do and say about encouraging and nurturing family involvement. Participation in this process exposes preservice teachers to the skills and benefits of "reflective practice." In addition, knowledge of how community members and agencies may partner with schools and families in the education of children is increasingly shown to be an important aspect of learning to teach (Grinberg & Goldfarb, 1998). Field experiences within the community enable preservice teachers to learn important information about community diversity, culture, and resources (Young & Edwards, 1996). Opportunities to reflect on issues surrounding teaching and family involvement within a community context enable preservice teachers to practice the dynamics of reflective practice while learning how to establish viable partnerships in real contexts. This book provides well-defined directions for establishing and conducting a reflective early field experience program. General guidelines for early field experiences appear in Appendix C.

REFERENCES

Bailey, D., Simeonsson, R., Yoder, D., & Huntington, G. (1990). Preparing professionals to serve infants and toddlers with handicaps and their families: An integrative analysis across eight disciplines. *Exceptional Children, 57*(1), 26–35.

Ball, D. L., Lambert, M., & Rosenberg, M. (1991, April). *Using hypermedia to investigate and construct knowledge about mathematics teaching and learning.* Paper presented at the annual meeting of the American Educational Research Association, Chicago.

Borko, H. & Putnam, R. (2000, January/February). What do new views of knowledge and thinking have to say about research on teacher learning? *Educational Researcher, 29*(1), 4–15.

Borko, H., & Putnam, R. T. (1996). Learning to teach. In D. C. Berliner & R. C. Calfee (Eds.), *Handbook of educational psychology* (pp. 673–708). New York: Macmillan.

Brophy, J. E. (1988). Research on teacher effects; uses and abuses. *Elementary School Journal, 89,* 3–21.

Brophy, J. E., & Good, T. L. (1986). Teacher behavior and student achievement. In M. C. Wittrock (Ed.), *Handbook of research on teaching* (3rd ed., pp. 328–375). New York: Macmillan.

Cazden, C. B. (1981). Social context of learning to read. In J. T. Guthrie (Ed.), *Comprehension and teaching: Research reviews* (pp. 118–139). Newark, DE: International Reading Association.

Diss, R. E., & Kolenbrander, R. W. (1993). What are teacher education students learning from early field experiences? *SRATE Journal, 2*(1), 34–39.

Doyle, W. (1990). Case methods in teacher education. *Teacher Education Quarterly, 17*(1), 7–15.

Evans-Schilling, D. (1996). Preparing educators for family involvement: Reflections, research and renewal. *Forum of Education, 51*(1), 35–46.

Farkas, S., Johnson, J., & Duffett, A. (1999). Playing their parts: Parents and teachers talk about parental involvement in public schools. In S. Farkas, J. Johnson, T. Foleno, A. Dufett, & P. Foley, *A sense of calling: Who teaches and why.* New York: Public Agenda, 2000.

Feltovich, P. J., Spiro, R. J., & Coulson, R. L. (1997). Issues of expert flexibility in contexts characterized by complexity and change. In P. J. Feltovich, K. M. Ford, & R. R. Hoffman (Eds.), *Expertise in context: Human and machine* (pp. 125–146). Cambridge, MA: MIT Press; Menlo Park, CA: AAAI Press.

Gold, Y. (1996). Beginning teacher support: Attrition, mentoring, and induction. In J. Sikula, T. J. Buttery, & E. Guyton (Eds.), *Handbook of research on teacher education* (2nd ed.). New York: Macmillan.

Grinberg, J., & Goldfarb, K. P., (1998). Moving teacher education into the community. *Theory into Practice, 37*(2), 131–139.

Greeno, J. G. (1997). On claims that answer the wrong questions. *Educational Researcher, 26*(1), 5–17.

Greeno, J. G., & the Middle School through Applications Project Group. (1998). The situativity of knowing, learning, and research. *American Psychologist, 53,* 5–26.

Guy, M. J. (Ed). (1993). *Teachers and teacher education: Essays on the national education goals* (Teacher Education Monograph No. 16). Washington, DC: ERIC Clearinghouse on Teacher Education, American Association of Colleges for Teacher Education.

Harvard Family Research Project. (1997). *New skills for new schools: Preparing teachers in family involvement.* Cambridge, MA: Harvard Graduate School of Education.

Henderson, A. T., & Berla, N. (1994). *A new generation of evidence: The family is critical to student achievement.* Columbia, MD: National Committee for Citizens in Education.

Kendall, E. D. (1993). Family and school coalitions: Surmounting obstacles. In M. J. Guy (Ed.), *Teachers and teacher education: Essays on the national education goals* (Teacher Education Monograph No. 16, pp. 21–34). Washington, DC: ERIC Clearinghouse on Teacher Education, American Association of Colleges for Teacher Education.

Kersh, M. E. (1995). Coordinating theory with practice. In G. A. Slick, (Ed.), *The field experience: Creating successful programs for new teachers.* Thousand Oaks, CA: Corwin Press.

McNamara, D. (1995). The influence of student teachers' tutors and mentors upon their classroom practice: An exploratory study. *Teaching and Teacher Education, 11,* 51–61.

Merseth, K. K. (1996). Cases and case methods in teacher education. In J. Sikula (Ed.), *Handbook of research on teacher education* (pp. 722–744). New York: MacMillan.

National PTA. (1998). *National standards for parent/family involvement programs.* Chicago: Author. Available from National PTA Web site, http://www.pta.org/programs/invstand.htm

Posner, G. J. (1995). *Field experience: A guide to reflective teaching* (4th ed.). New York: Longman.

Putnam, J. G. (1984). *One exceptional teacher's systematic decision-making model* (Research Series No. 136). East Lansing: Michigan State University, Institute for Research on Teaching.

Schon, D. A. (1983). *The reflective practitioner.* San Francisco: Jossey-Bass.

Shulman, L. (1987). Knowledge and teaching: Foundation of the new reform. *Harvard Educational Review, 51,* 1–22.

U.S. Department of Education. (1994). *Strong families, strong schools: Building community partnerships for learning.* Washington, DC: U.S. Government Printing Office.

Wasserman, S. (1994). *Getting down to cases: Learning to teach with case studies.* New York: Teachers College Press.

Wildman, T. M., & Niles, J. A. (1987). Essentials of professional growth. *Educational Leadership, 44*(5), 4–10.

Winton, P. J., & DiVenere, N. (1995). Family-professional partnerships in early intervention personnel preparation: Guidelines and strategies. *Topics in Early Childhood Special Education, 15,* 296–313.

Young, L. S. J., & Edwards, P. A. (1996). Parents, families, and communities: Opportunities for preservice teacher education. In F. B. Murray (Ed.), *The teacher educator's handbook.* San Francisco: Jossey-Bass.

1

THE CONTEMPORARY
AMERICAN FAMILY

Teachers must have a realistic understanding of the diverse and complex nature of contemporary families if they expect to establish and maintain effective home–school–community partnerships.

Ronald E. Diss and Pamela K. Buckley

In the 1950s the typical American family included a father, mother, and two children. By 1978 a change in family structure was well on the way. Today there is no typical American family. No single definition of *family*, no matter how broad, covers the variety of relational groupings characteristic of families today. The U.S. Census Bureau (1998) defines *family* as a household that has at least two members related by "blood, marriage, or adoption." This definition obviously does not account for the many organizational patterns of family that are common today. Families can be comprised of members who are not related by birth, marriage, or adoption, and many families have members who do not live in the same house. From a sociological perspective, the definition of *family* appropriately may include a group of individuals who are bonded together by common goals and who support, help, and care for one another.

In today's world, teachers must be prepared to relate to students and their caregivers from a variety of family structures, including intact, blended, single-parent, and nontraditional families headed by foster parents, grandparents, older siblings, aunts and uncles, or same-gender partners. Likewise, social, economic, and cultural factors have brought about a change in the profile of the American family. All of these change factors influence the lives of today's children in significant ways and define who they are. To understand students, teachers must understand the families from which they come. This understanding will enable teachers to help family members play a larger role in their child's learning.

PROFILE OF THE CONTEMPORARY AMERICAN FAMILY

The TV series *Boston Public* reflects the reality of a typical inner-city school in a large, urban area with a highly diverse student population. Students and teachers face issues related to drugs, gang wars, drive-by shootings, unwanted pregnancies, eating disorders, homelessness, and parental abuse. Parents in the series include those who are divorced, mentally ill, uninvolved, homeless,

11

middle class, upper income, and impoverished. There are as many variations on parents as there are students. Parent involvement is limited to conferences at the school in which the principal or a concerned teacher tells the parent about a serious problem the student has. In several episodes the teacher visits a student's home to investigate possible abuse. Although the events in this television series take place in an inner-city urban environment, they reflect what is occurring on a somewhat smaller scale in suburban and rural areas.

The themes treated in *Boston Public* illustrate clearly a significant aspect of understanding families and schools; that is, how personal and environmental circumstances combine to influence and create the complex contexts in which individuals, families, and schools function and must be understood. This "ecological" or "systems" theory, advanced by Bronfenbrenner (Bronfenbrenner, 1986; Bronfenbrenner & Morris, 1998), explains how the dominant beliefs and ideologies of society both influence and are influenced by individuals, families, schools, and the broader community. Bronfenbrenner's theory is applied in Chapter 5 to demonstrate how various social structures may influence behavior and, therefore, the nature of home–school partnerships.

SIGNIFICANT AREAS OF CHANGE

In *Home-School Relations*, Fuller and Olsen (1998) identify four factors influencing families: (1) family structures; (2) ethnic, racial, and cultural backgrounds; (3) available income; and (4) individual family differences. The following discussion is organized around Fuller and Olsen's four factors.

FAMILY STRUCTURES

What changes have occurred in American families in the last 25 years? According to recent data on population and family characteristics (Federal Interagency Forum on Child and Family Statistics, 2001), it has become more common for a child to come from a nontraditional family structure. The number of families in which there is no spouse present, but with other relatives including children, has increased from 11% of all households in 1970 to 16% in 2000 (U.S. Census Bureau, 2000). Contemporary nonnuclear family structures include single-parent families, same-gender families, reconstructed families (stepfamilies), families headed by family members other than parents, and foster care families (Coontz, 1995; Fuller & Marxen, 1998). *National Vital Statistics Report* for February 2000 indicates that births to women in their 40s and early 50s have risen (Martin, Hamilton, Ventura, Menacker, & Park, 2002). The increasing age among first-time parents, and the trend toward older women giving birth have resulted in an older parent population than in the past.

In the year 2000, 69% of American children lived with two parents. Among children living with two parents, 91% lived with biological or adoptive parents and 9% lived with a biological or adoptive parent and a stepparent. Twenty-two percent lived with only their mothers, 4% lived with only their fathers, and 4% lived with neither of their parents (Federal Interagency Forum on Child and

What is a family? What criteria should be used to determine the definition of family?

Family Statistics, 2001). Four fifths of children living with a stepparent lived with their mother and a stepfather.

Statistics show that the majority of children living with one parent live with their single mother. Between 1970 and 1997, the number of one-parent families in the United States increased by 216% (U.S. Bureau of the Census, 1998). Eighty-three percent of those families were headed by mothers and 17% were headed by fathers. High divorce and illegitimacy rates suggest that both the number and total percentage of these families will continue to increase. For example, in 1999, 33% of all births were to unmarried mothers (U.S. Bureau of the Census, 1998). Increases in births to unmarried women are among the many changes in American society that have affected family structure.

More children are being reared by grandparents or other family members. Among the 2.6 million children not living with either parent in 1996, half lived with grandparents, whereas about 21% lived with other relatives, and another 22% lived with nonrelatives. Of children in nonrelatives' homes, about half lived with foster parents (Federal Interagency Forum on Child and Family Statistics, 2001). These figures are important because the number of parents living with a child generally is linked to the amount and quality of human and economic resources available to that child.

With the trend toward nontraditional family structures, teachers can expect to see a full range of family situations in their classrooms. However, as stated, the most common contemporary family structure is the one-parent family. The two largest categories of children of one-parent families are those headed by an unmarried mother and single-parent homes created by divorce (Ahlburg & De Vita, 1992; Tutwiler, 1998). The one-parent family, therefore, represents a major segment of the population, especially among African American and low-income families. In 1997, 52% of all African American children under the age of 18 lived with a single mother, as compared with 18% of White children and 28% of Hispanic children (U.S. Bureau of the Census, 1998).

What are the implications of the one-parent family for the classroom teacher? Teachers will encounter less parental support and direct communication with the school than in years past. Many single-parent families are struggling to cope with harsh economic realities and barely manage to provide for basic needs of the family. Job and household responsibilities tend to receive priority over any type of meaningful involvement with the school.

ETHNIC, RACIAL, AND CULTURAL BACKGROUNDS

Today, families in America represent an increasingly diverse, multiethnic population. Consequently, K–12 students come from a wide range of cultures. Of the 51 million elementary and secondary students enrolled in American schools in 1997, approximately 64.2% were White, and 35% were minorities (Snyder, 1999). Among this minority population, 16.9% were African American, 14% were Hispanic, 3.8% were Asian/Pacific American, and 1.1% were American Indian/Aleut/Alaskan Native. The 2000 census figures indicate that the number of Hispanics is now greater than the number of African Americans. Thus, the ethnic and racial composition of American schools continues to change rapidly. By the year 2010, over two thirds of the students enrolled in U.S. public schools are anticipated to be members of an ethnic minority group (Meece, 2002). In addition to cultural diversity, non-Judeo-Christian religions such as Buddhism, Hinduism, and Islam are adding new dimensions to classrooms (Tutwiler, 1998).

What are the implications of the growing diversity in the student population for the classroom teacher? Teachers face tremendous challenges in involving all families. Alarmingly, teachers today are predominantly from White middle-class families with little experience with diverse cultures (Blackwell, 2001; Darling-Hammond & Sclan, 1997; Fuller, 1994; Webb & Sherman, 1989; Zimpher, 1996). Many new teachers will not have had an opportunity to come to terms with cultural differences, to examine their own personal biases, to acquire skills that help students of cultures different from their own, and to appreciate the unique strengths and needs of other cultures. This lack of preparation for multicultural teaching is known to be an impediment to student success (Mason, 1999; Moore, 1996; Schrag, 1999).

AVAILABLE INCOME

Even though figures may vary according to community, nearly 25% of children born in the United States today live in poverty (Children's Defense Fund, 2000). Traditionally, poverty status is assigned to families based on household income

Do some common school activities fail to reflect the realities of the contemporary family? What are some of these practices?

compared to the federal poverty threshold figure reflecting the estimated cost of food for a basic diet of family members multiplied by 3 (Huston, McLoyd, & McColl, 1994). The poverty rate for children is even higher among families living in rural areas, especially among African American and Mexican American children (Edelman, 1997). Santrock (1998, 2001) profiles further dimensions of poor children in the United States in the following statistical breakdown of every 100 children living in poverty in America:

40	are White, non-Latino.
34	are African American.
22	are Latino.
37	live in married-couple families.
59	live in female-headed families.
4	live in male-headed families.
62	live in families with at least one worker.
17	live in families with two or more workers.
22	live in families with at least one full-time, year-round worker.
45	live in central cities.
32	live in suburban areas.
24	live in rural areas.

44	live in families with incomes of less than half the poverty level ($6,962.00 for a family of four).
40	are younger than 6.
11	live in families headed by a person younger than 25.[1]

Additionally, the most recent estimate of homeless U.S. citizens is seven million, with children constituting 15% of this number (U.S. Department of Education, 1997). These figures do not take into account the large number of extremely vulnerable individuals who are on the edge of homelessness. There are approximately three million families on public housing waiting lists (U.S. Department of Housing and Urban Development, Interagency Council on Homelessness, 1994).

INDIVIDUAL FAMILY DIFFERENCES

Although families have many things in common, they all have individual differences that make them unique. Their histories and characteristics define who they are as a family. One of the characteristics that accounts for a significant difference in some families is having a child who qualifies for special education services. Parents of children who qualify for these services tend to be highly involved in their children's education. This is largely due to federal laws since 1976 that protect the rights of all children from birth through age 21 to receive a free, appropriate public education in the least restrictive environment (U.S. Department of Education, 1996). The enforcement and implementation of these laws has educated families about the guaranteed educational rights of all children and the many programs available to accommodate their needs. Thus, parents of children with special needs generally play active roles advocating for quality programs for their children. A common expectation today is the inclusion of children with special needs into the regular classroom. All educators must understand the needs of these children and their families if they are to establish a parent–teacher partnership based on mutual respect and participation in decision making.

CONCLUSION

Whereas families differ in structure, culture, ethnicity, and economic situations, all parents have the welfare of their children at heart. They want their children to do well in school and become successful in life. Communicating with and involving families reflecting a wide variety of family conditions and structures presents a significant challenge to teachers. Teachers must be knowledgeable about their students and the homes from which they come if they are to involve families in meeting their children's learning needs. To establish successful home–school partnerships, teachers need to understand the diverse backgrounds of their students and the opportunities for involvement that these diverse backgrounds afford. The remaining chapters in this text explore these issues in greater detail.

---

[1]From *Child Development* (p. 583), by J. W. Santrock, 1998, New York: McGraw-Hill. Reproduced with permission of The McGraw-Hill Companies.

APPLICATION
Working with Families

What are some strategies for building positive relationships with families? Teachers, school administrators, and other personnel must be sensitive to family structures, cultural diversity, ethnicity, and economic situations. As we have noted, many children come from nontraditional family structures. Don't assume that a child lives with both parents, or even a mother or father. Ask before you call the parents or send notes home to "Mom and Dad." Also, don't assume that the child's family speaks and reads English. Older children can translate written materials for their parents, but early primary school students may not be able to. Try to determine the primary language spoken in the home and seek translators from the community, if necessary, to help make connections through telephone calls to the home or in written communication.

Remember that today's classrooms reflect a more diverse population with a number of different cultures and ethnic groups. Be informed about major religious holidays and traditions of different groups and note special days on any calendars displayed in the classroom. Ask students to share information about special celebrations and cultural events their families observe.

When assigning homework, consider the environments in which students may be working. Don't assume that homework is a priority for all families. Students in homes where both parents hold full-time jobs may not be able to get a ride to the library to do research. Students in single-parent homes may have responsibilities for younger siblings and housekeeping chores that leave little time for schoolwork. Students in impoverished homes may not have access to computers or resource materials. Homeless students living in shelters may not have a quiet area in which they can concentrate. It would be helpful to meet with other teachers to negotiate a balance in homework assignments among the different classes. Collaborate with teachers of other disciplines to integrate curriculum assignments. For example, a Civil War unit might include completing maps, writing a letter home from a soldier's viewpoint, and solving math problems related to transporting supplies. Teachers might want to exchange suggestions about the types of assignments that seem to offer the best potential for being completed.

Share your expectations for family support through telephone calls or notes sent home. Let families know how they can participate in their child's learning. Inform them of resources in the community that are available to support their parenting.

The case study that follows concerns a single parent and the challenges she faces in rearing her children. Family circumstances have created an environment in which the young son is disruptive in school as well as at home. The parent and the teacher experience a conflict because they each have differing expectations for the other's roles and responsibilities. The names of the characters have been changed, but the situation is based on an actual event. As a teacher, you are likely to encounter similar situations.

Dedra is the single parent of Damien, a first grader, and his half sister Tameka, a junior in high school. Dedra receives no financial support from Damien's father, who has never lived with the family but who visits Damien about twice a year. Damien's teacher has called Dedra at her job telling her that she must come to school immediately to take Damien home. For the fifth time in 3 weeks, Damien has violated a "level three" school rule which, according to the school's discipline plan, carries the consequence of school suspension following a parent conference.

This time Damien violated the school's discipline plan by running away from the school playground during recess. Mrs. Jackson, Damien's teacher, reported the incident to Mr. Hobbs, the principal, who later found him six blocks away near the high school where he claimed he was going to find his sister Tameka. Mrs. Jackson, who admittedly has "just about had it" with Damien, has, in the past, reported to both Mr. Hobbs and Dedra that Damien hates school, won't do his work, disrupts and picks on his classmates, curses, steals, cheats, and destroys school property.

Damien has also been "written up" in previous weeks for urinating on the floor in the boy's bathroom, and for bringing pornography to school. Mrs. Jackson reports, however, that at times Damien can be "as sweet as an angel." Mrs. Jackson has asked Mr. Hobbs to support her efforts to get "Dedra's attention," and to get her involved in helping to "straighten Damien out" at school.

"Look, I'm doing the best I can. It's not easy raising two kids by myself, but I'm trying," said Dedra. "I'm working two shifts at the restaurant to keep my family together, and I need to keep this job. I lose money every time you call me to come to school when Damien gets into trouble. I might even be fired! This is the fifth time you've called me this month. Hey, I'm trying to do my job; can't you do yours? If you can't get Damien to behave in school, what am I supposed to do when I'm not even here? You're the professionals who have the training to deal with kids in school, so don't expect me to do your jobs. You take care of Damien; when he's in school, he's your job."

Damien's mom continued, "I've had my share of problems at home with him, too. God knows, he's no angel. His older sister Tameka tries her best to give him the attention he needs after school and on weekends until I get home from work, but she can only do so much. He doesn't have anyone his own age to play with where we live, so he gets mixed up with those older boys. Last week they put him up to stealing candy from the 7-11 and the manager caught him. So, now he's grounded and giving Tameka fits. It's not fair that she's got to stay home with him all the time, either. What am I supposed to do, beat him? God knows, that won't work; that boy's suffered enough as it is in his short life. I think he's mad at me because he don't see his daddy but two or three times a year. Last week he said he hated me and that he felt like running away because I was so mean to him. So, we've all got problems with Damien—you've got yours, and I've got mine. If I could help you, I would, and if you'd quit calling me away from my job it sure would help me."

CASE STUDY DISCUSSION GUIDE

Themes: The impact of school rules and consequences on family life; the impact of the home environment on school behavior; maintaining appropriate school environments; division of roles and responsibilities; and home–school collaboration.

Actors

A. How would you characterize each of the actors in this case? (List each person's name and give one-, two-, or three-word descriptions for each actor.)

Probes

1. How do you think each of the actors in this case feels?
2. How does Dedra view her responsibility for her son's school behavior?
3. How does Mrs. Jackson view Dedra's responsibility for her son's school behavior?
4. What kind of principal is Mr. Hobbs?
5. What kind of parent is Dedra?

Issues

B. What are the major issues in this case? (Make a list of these issues.)

Probes

1. Is the school justified in having strict school rules and consequences? Why or why not?
2. Is Damien's mother justified in her claim that the school is responsible for dealing with Damien while he is at school? Why or why not?
3. Who needs help in this case? What kind of help?
4. To what extent are school personnel expected to become involved in the lives of students?
5. Should school personnel be held equally responsible for the learning achievement of all children regardless of their home backgrounds?

Problems or Conflicts

C. What are the major problems or conflicts in this case? Make a list of these problems or conflicts and specify whether you think they stem from personal or institutional origins. Now, examine the list further. Can they be organized into primary and secondary categories? (After completing this last step, you may find it easier to suggest solutions to the problems or conflicts in this case.)

Probes

1. Who is upset at whom? Why?
2. What does each actor want to achieve?

Solutions

D. How could the problems or conflicts in this case have been prevented? If you had been one of the actors in this case, what would you have done differently?

Probes

1. How can all parties work together to resolve the conflicts in this case to everyone's benefit? (List what each person could do.)
2. What community agencies might be of help to Dedra?

SUPPLEMENTAL ACTIVITIES

The following activities include two types of field experiences: a school-based activity and a community-based activity. The school activity can be done as you complete your early field experiences that require observations at a school site. The community activity is designed to acquaint you with social service agencies that provide family support and resources. Appendix A includes suggestions for community resources, and Appendix C contains detailed directions for participant observations.

FIELD EXPERIENCE A

School-Based Activity

As you observe in schools, look for behaviors, events, and activities that reflect school expectations or policies regarding the treatment of disruptive or noncompliant student behavior. Ask school personnel how they routinely involve parents when their children get into trouble at school. You may want to focus your inquiries and observations on one or more of the following questions:

1. What is the school's policy regarding noncompliant student behavior? Are there schoolwide rules? What are these rules? Are there specified consequences applied when particular rules are broken? What are these consequences? Are the consequences applied equally?

2. In addition to schoolwide rules, most teachers establish "classroom rules" to direct student behavior during instruction. How do teachers establish these rules? Is there a procedure for teachers to follow when making up their classroom rules to ensure appropriateness? If there is such a procedure, what is it?

3. How are schoolwide and classroom rules and consequences for noncompliant behavior communicated to students and parents? How do school personnel ensure that these communication efforts are effective?

4. What options do school personnel have in place for involving parents to ensure that school rules are obeyed?

5. Knowing that family structures vary considerably, are there options in place to accommodate the involvement of parents heading nontraditional households to help their children support school rules? If so, what are these options?

6. Are parents included in decisions about school rules and consequences? If so, in what ways are they involved?

7. What recourse do students and parents have when disagreements about noncompliant behavior or punishment occur?

Community-Based Activity

Interview the principal and the school guidance counselor (if there is one) to see what types of resources are available to parents in the community. Do any agencies offer financial resources to assist families in need? Do any agencies offer counseling in parenting skills? Is there a federally funded parent center in the school that offers training in parenting skills? Are there agencies that provide afterschool programs to children like Damien to see that he has constructive activities during his out-of-school time? Are there Big Brother or Big Sister programs to provide mentoring to neighborhood children? Prepare an annotated list of these agencies and their services to present to the school if one doesn't already exist. Call or visit as many of these agencies as time permits to learn more about their services and success rates. You may want to focus your inquiries and observations on one or more of the following questions:

1. What types of resources are available to families?

2. How do agencies let potential clients know about their services?

3. Are the services provided on a sliding fee scale?

4. Do any of the agencies focus on helping parents communicate more effectively with the school?

As an alternative to using the "Case Study Discussion Guide," you may want to reflect on the case and construct a written response to the following prompts:

1. Knowing the circumstances of this case, how would you respond to the following comments made by Dedra? "Hey, I'm trying to do my job; can't you do yours?" "If you can't get Damien to behave in school, what am I supposed to do when I'm not even here? You're the professionals who have the training to deal with kids in school, so don't expect me to do your jobs. You take care of Damien; when he's in school, he's your job."

2. Describe the kind of support you think Dedra needs to receive from Damien's school. If Damien and his family have needs that cannot be served by the school, does the school's responsibility cease? Explain your answer.

3. Make a list of school and community resources that you think may be available to Damien's family.

4. If you had been Damien's teacher, how would you have handled the situation?

Role play being a single working parent trying hard to raise an unruly child with little assistance from family members. You may want to assume the characters portrayed in "Who's Responsible for Damien?" As the roles are acted out, observers will want to take notes on their perceptions about how to balance the need for teachers and administrators to ensure appropriate school behavior, while also respecting student and family differences.

Following the role playing, participants may want to group themselves according to the grade level at which they anticipate teaching. Each group's task will be to construct a list of classroom rules and consequences for breaking these rules. Make sure that the rules and consequences for noncompliance include how administrators and parents will be involved in supporting appropriate student behavior.

DISCUSSION
After completing the group task, each group may want to share their lists with the other groups and discuss differences.

Following the role-playing activity, construct a list of implications for family involvement related to school and classroom rules. You may want to modify your lists after listening to the comments and insights of your classmates.

REFERENCES

Ahlburg, D. A., & De Vita, C. (1992). New realities of the American family. *Population Bulletin, 47*(2).

Bronfenbrenner U. (1986). Ecology of the family as a context for human development: Research perspectives. *Developmental Psychology, 22*(6), 723–742.

Bronfenbrenner, U., & Morris, P. (1998). The ecology of developmental processes. In R. Lermer (Ed.), *Handbook of Child Psychology: Theoretical models of human development* (5th ed., Vol. 1, pp. 993–1028). New York: Wiley.

Blackwell, P. J. (2001). *The jigsaw puzzle of teacher education.* Washington, DC: U.S. Department of Education, Office of Educational Research and Development.

Children's Defense Fund. (2000). *Yearbook 2000: The state of America's children.* Washington, DC: Author.

Coontz, S. (1995). The American family and the nostalgia trap. *Phi Delta Kappan, 76*(7), K1–K20.

Darling-Hammond, L., & Sclan, E. M. (1997). Who teaches and why: Dilemmas of building a profession for twenty-first century schools. In J. Sikula, T. J. Buttery, & E. Guyton, (Eds.), *Handbook of research on teacher education* (2nd ed.). New York: Macmillan.

Edelman, M. W. (1997, April). *Children, families and social policy.* Paper presented at the meeting of the Society for Research in Child Development, Washington, DC.

Federal Interagency Forum on Child and Family Statistics. (2001). *America's children: Key national indicators of well-being*. Available from Child Stats.gov Web site, http://www.childstats.gov

Fuller, M. L. (1994). The monocultural graduate in a multicultural environment: A challenge to teacher education. *Journal of Teacher Education, 43*(4), 269–278.

Fuller, M. L., & Marxen, C. (1998). Families and their functions—Past and present. In M. L. Fuller, & G. Olsen, (Eds.), *Home-School relations* (pp. 11–39). Boston: Allyn & Bacon.

Fuller, M. L., & Olsen, G. (Eds.) (1998). *Home-school relations*. Boston: Allyn & Bacon.

Huston, A. C., McLoyd, V. C., & McColl, C. G. (1994). Children and poverty: Issues in contemporary research. *Child Development, 65*, 275–282.

Martin, J., Hamilton, B., Ventura, S., Menacker, F., & Park, M. Births: Final data for 2000. (2002). *National Vital Statistics Report, 50*(5). Washington, DC: Centers for Disease Control and Prevention.

Mason, T. C. (1999). Prospective teachers' attitudes toward urban schools: Can they be changed? *Multicultural Education, 6*(4), 9–13.

Meece, J. L. (2002). *Child and adolescent development for educators* (2nd ed., p. 215). Boston: McGraw-Hill.

Moore, J. A. (1996). *Empowering student teachers to teach from a multicultural perspective*. Paper presented at the Annual Meeting of the American Association of Colleges for Teacher Education, Chicago. (ERIC Document Reproduction Service No. ED394979)

Santrock, J. W. (1998). *Child development* (8th ed., p. 583). Boston: McGraw-Hill.

Santrock, J. W. (2001). *Child development* (9th ed., p. 560). Boston: McGraw-Hill.

Schrag, P. (1999, July-August). Who will teach the teachers? *University Business*. Available from http://www.universitybusiness.com/9907/teach.html

Snyder, T. (1999). *Digest of education statistics, 1998*. Washington, DC: U.S. Department of Education.

Tutwiler, S. W. (1998). Diversity among families. In M. L. Fuller & G. Olsen (Eds.), *Home-school relations* (pp. 40–66). Boston: Allyn & Bacon.

U.S. Census Bureau. (1998). *Statistical abstract of the United States 1998*. Washington, DC: U.S. Government Printing Office, 1998.

U.S. Census Bureau. (2000). Census 2000 Gateway. Available from: www.census.gov/main/www/cen2000.html

U.S. Department of Education, Office of Special Education Programs. (1996). *Number and disabilities of children and youth served under IDEA*. Data Analysis System. Washington, DC: Author.

U.S. Department of Education. (1997). *Meeting the needs of homeless children and youth: A resource for schools and communities*. Washington, DC: Author.

U.S. Department of Housing and Urban Development, Interagency Council on Homelessness. (1994, March). *Priority, home!: The federal plan to break the cycle of homeless* (HUD-1454-CPD, pp. 17–36). Washington, DC: Author.

Webb, R. B., & Sherman, R. R. (1989). *Schooling and society* (2nd ed.). New York: Macmillan.

Zimpher, N. L. (1996). *Right-sizing teacher education: The policy initiative*. In L. Kaplan & R. A. Edelfelt (Eds.), *Teachers for the new millennium*. Thousand Oaks, CA: Corwin Press.

2

THE FAMILY'S ROLE
IN EDUCATION

Parents are the essential link in improving American education, and schools simply have to do a better job reaching out to them. Sending a report card home is not enough. Parents want to help their children succeed in school, and often need guidance on how to be most effective.

Richard W. Riley, former secretary, U.S. Department of Education, *Reaching All Families: Creating Family-Friendly Schools,* 1997

EFFECT OF FAMILY INVOLVEMENT ON STUDENT ACHIEVEMENT

What effect does family involvement have on student achievement? Many studies have produced strong evidence that active family involvement does indeed have an impact on student achievement (Booth & Dunn, 1996; Epstein, 1995; Hoover-Dempsey & Sandler, 1995, 1997). Studies of individual families show that what the family does is more important to student success than family income or education. This holds true whether the family is wealthy or impoverished, whether the parents finished high school or not, or whether the child is in preschool or in the upper grades (Coleman et al., 1966; Henderson & Berla, 1994; Keith & Keith, 1993; Olmstead & Rubin, 1983). The most comprehensive research conducted on the subject is a series of publications by Henderson and Berla: *The Evidence Grows* (1981), *The Evidence Continues to Grow* (Henderson, 1987), and *A New Generation of Evidence* (1994). Citing more than 85 studies, these publications document the profound and comprehensive benefits for students, families, and schools when parents and family members become active participants in their children's educations and lives.

Three factors over which parents exercise significant control—student absenteeism, the variety of reading materials in the home, and excessive television viewing—account for nearly 90% of the variations in eighth-grade mathematics test scores across 37 states and the District of Columbia on the National Assessment of Educational Progress (NAEP). Thus, home factors that parents can control account for almost all of the differences in average student achievement across states (Barton & Coley, 1992).

Educators agree that parent involvement is the most accurate predictor of student achievement regardless of economic, racial, or cultural background (Henderson & Berla, 1994). When parents and other family members share with teachers the role of educating children, everyone benefits. Children benefit because their chances of succeeding in school are dramatically increased. Parents benefit because they enjoy the success of their children, and see themselves as competent parents. Teachers benefit because they are more readily able to deliver instruction resulting in higher levels of student achievement. Put simply, parents play a significant role in the education of their children by preparing them with essential readiness learning skills, by communicating with teachers, by supporting classroom and school activities, and by providing afterschool structures that enable children to practice and reinforce the skills they learn in school.

At the same time, teachers must respect whatever level of involvement parents are able to provide. Some parents will not be able to volunteer assistance in the classroom or attend school functions because of employment or family responsibilities. Other parents may be too preoccupied with personal problems to become involved in their child's education. Thus, teachers should show appreciation to parents who are helping their children at home, even if all they are able to do is encourage the children to do their homework.

Parents play an important role in the education of their children. Student achievement is significantly higher when parents show support for, and are involved in, their children's learning and school activities.

What do existing patterns of family involvement tell us about establishing effective home–school partnerships? General patterns of involvement suggest that the younger the children are the more involved parents tend to be. Typically, children in the primary grades have the highest levels of family involvement. Also, affluent families tend to be more positively involved in their children's schooling than low-income families are, especially when headed by one parent (Collins, Dewees, & Togneri, 1999). Families whose cultures are different from the mainstream American culture are also less involved in school activities than their American counterparts (Christensen, 1992; Fan & Chen, 1999).

Studies conducted by the Center on Families, Communities, Schools, and Children's Learning (1994) indicate that parents who receive frequent and positive messages from teachers tend to become more involved in their children's education. The families of children attending schools in economically disadvantaged localities tend to receive more negative communication from school personnel than do families of children attending schools in better neighborhoods. Additionally, families tend to be more involved in home–school partnerships when there are two parents in the household, when parents work in the home, and when parents live near the school (Ames, De Stefano, Watkins, & Sheldon, 1995). These three factors relate to the resource of time. When two parents are available to become involved in a child's education, there is more time for one or both to communicate with the school and to participate in activities. Parents who work in the home have more flexible schedules and may be easier to contact. Parents who live near the school may find it easier to drop by for meetings or activities in the morning or afternoon on their way to and from work.

Research indicates that mothers in two-parent families are much more involved in school activities than are fathers (Cooksey & Fondell, 1996; Thomson, McLanahan, & Curtin, 1992); however, single fathers and mothers are as highly involved as mothers in two-parent families (U.S. Department of Education, 1997). Regardless of whether children live in two-parent or in single-parent families, the proportion of children whose mothers or fathers are highly involved in their schools increases as their parents' education level increases (U.S. Department of Education, 1996).

Unfortunately, many teachers and families often think of family involvement as primarily mothers' involvement. Historically, this assumption is probably correct because mothers in two-parent families have been more likely than fathers to be highly involved in their children's schools (Cooksey & Fondell, 1996; Thomson et al., 1992). Even though mothers' involvement is strongly related to children's school achievement, research indicates that students also do better in school when their fathers are involved (Swick, 1984; Swick & Manning, 1983; U.S. Department of Education, 1997.) It is interesting to note that fathers and mothers who head single-parent families are virtually identical in their pattern of involvement in their children's schools (Nord, Brimhall, & West, 1997). Therefore, it would seem that as schools strive to increase levels of parental involvement, they would do well

A traditional way to involve parents and other family members in school activities is to depend on them to help raise money for the school. While this is important to many school programs, this kind of involvement is quite limited. What other kinds of family involvement activities can you suggest?

to reach out to the families of children of all age groups, ethnic and cultural backgrounds, economic levels, and fathers in two-parent households.

OPPORTUNITIES FOR EXPANDING FAMILY INVOLVEMENT

Most educators expect parents and other family members to contribute to their children's education by providing service to the school, getting their children socially and intellectually ready for school, supporting school programs, and reinforcing learning at home. Traditionally, school personnel have encouraged these activities as excellent opportunities for parents to demonstrate their role as the child's primary educator.

Although existing patterns of family involvement indicate many positive home–school relationships benefiting many students, additional opportunities for involvement and greater levels of participation are needed. These opportunities must accommodate the needs of families who have conflicting work schedules, language barriers, cultural expectations, and negative attitudes about the school environment. A strong parental involvement program works to make the school welcoming to all parents and develops a variety of ways to engage parents in the education of their children.

Epstein and colleagues identify six types of involvement to accommodate a wide variety of family needs (Epstein, Coates, Salinas, Sanders, & Simon, 1997). These types include communicating, parenting, volunteering, learning at home, school decision making, and collaborating with the community. These types, or categories of involvement, also serve as the basis for the six national standards for parent or family involvement programs adopted by the National Parent Teacher Association (PTA; National PTA, 1998).

The following discussion is organized around Epstein's six types of parent or family involvement.

1. **Communicating:** Children benefit most when there is regular and meaningful two-way communication between home and school. Family members need to listen to teachers, and teachers need to listen to family members to arrive at mutually supportive ways to send the clear message to children that both are working together to help them succeed in school. Two-way communications invite families and teachers to work as partners because they are able to share reactions, ideas, preferences, and questions about needs, expectations, programs, and children's progress.

2. **Parenting:** When family members spend time with young children at home, playing and interacting with them, reading to them, and exposing them to the world of life, they stimulate their learning readiness. *America's Kindergartners*, a report released by the U.S. Department of Education's National Center for Education Statistics (NCES; West, Denton, & Germino-Hausken, 2000), provides first-time national data on 22,000 children attending public and private kindergarten, their families, and their classrooms. The study found that most of the nation's children enter school with strong learning readiness skills: Nearly all, 94%, can count to 10 and pick out shapes. Two in three know their ABCs. More than 80% make friends, cooperate, and otherwise avoid bad behavior. All but 3% are in good health.

Although the findings were positive for the population as a whole, there are several groups of children whose knowledge and skills put them at risk. Children living in poverty, those from single-parent and non–English-speaking homes, and those whose parents didn't finish high school were less likely to count to 10 or recite the alphabet or to be in good health. Many primary caregivers may benefit from programs and activities that provide information on children's health, safety, nutrition, topics associated with development during childhood and adolescence, and ways to condition the home to support learning at each grade level, including homework, punctuality, and following school rules. These activities may also increase the school's understanding of families by initiating programs to promote exchanges of information between home and school about their shared care and concerns for children.

3. **Volunteering:** Traditionally, families have viewed parent involvement as an opportunity to provide service to the school. These activities commonly have included baking cookies, monitoring parties, preparing bulletin boards, chaperoning field trips, raising funds, and providing secretarial service to teachers. When families participate in these service-type opportunities to be

Reading to children from their earliest years helps to establish important learning skills. In addition to reading to children, what else can parents do to help them develop learning skills?

involved in the school's programs, they strengthen those programs by providing needed services, show support for their child's schooling, and communicate to their children that going to school is a valued priority.

Although these activities are useful to both school and family because they contribute to student motivation which leads to increased achievement, they are limited in scope; true home–school partnerships must actively involve parents in decision making and more substantial aspects of the school's mission.

4. **Student Learning at Home:** Parents can support schools by reading to their young children, providing a variety of reading materials at home, taking their children to the library, monitoring television viewing, providing a quiet place to do homework, encouraging children's school efforts, and staying in touch with their children's teachers. Family members can play a significant role in providing opportunities at home for children to practice learned skills. Such activity is commonly associated with "homework" assignments. When family members provide the structure at home for children to reinforce what they learned at school, they provide an essential support that enables them to retain and accelerate their learning.

Helping students with their homework also provides family members with information about what students are learning, allows them to participate directly in that learning, and encourages interaction among family members about their knowledge and experiences related to students' schoolwork.

5. **School Decision Making and Advocacy:** Teachers can encourage parental support by making them feel welcome in the school; accommodating parents' work schedules when designing parent involvement activities; assigning meaningful homework assignments that engage each child's family; and keeping parents informed of their children's progress through notes, telephone calls, newsletters, conferences, and meetings. When family members are invited to participate in decisions about school programs that affect their own children, they are able to feel confident that their voices are heard and that programs reflect the needs of their children. This involvement helps to ensure that the family will support school activities by reinforcing the value of these programs to their children and encouraging their participation. It is also important to keep in mind that these supportive family members share their enthusiasm for school involvement with other parents and patrons of the school, creating significant opportunities for increased awareness, support, and participation of the broader community.

6. **Collaborating with Community:** In addition to families and schools, community members play a significant role in the education of young people. Within communities, there are many resources (human, economic, material, and social) that can support and enhance home and school involvement. The identification and integration of these resources improves schools, strengthens families, and assists students to succeed in school (Epstein et al., 1997). Ideas for learning about community involvement programs are given in the **Application** section of each chapter. See Appendix A for community involvement resources.

NEGATIVE ASPECTS OF INVOLVEMENT PROGRAMS

Is there a negative side to school involvement programs? Some school personnel would respond with a resounding "yes" to this question, citing various problems associated with welcoming family and community members into the school. Whereas these problems may be real, the authors prefer to look at them as challenges and opportunities to improve the school's program. Perhaps the greatest challenge presented by involvement programs is the fear that they will distract school personnel from doing their jobs. Schools are complex and oftentimes unpredictable environments; they are busy places where numerous activities unfold every day involving large numbers of people. These activities are intended to deliver the school's instructional program. By establishing school routines and procedures, administrators and teachers hope to reduce the unpredictability of the school environment and, therefore, better ensure the achievement of school goals. Some school personnel worry that when family and community members become involved, the school environment becomes

Due to family circumstances, some caregivers find it extremely difficult to help children with homework. Some localities have afterschool programs which include scheduled time to receive help with homework. How else might community agencies assist parents and schools in educating children and youth?

more complex, resulting in less predictability and threatening the achievement of instructional goals. On the contrary, when involvement programs are well prepared and integrated as an integral part of the school's program, they enable volunteers to offer critical assistance to school personnel working to achieve school goals.

Another challenge of involvement programs is the fact that implementing successful programs requires a commitment of time and effort to see them to fruition. As Chapter 7 illustrates, successful involvement programs don't just happen, they are the result of the efforts of many people over time to achieve planned program goals. Time must be allocated to achieve these goals. Even a relatively small item, such as preparing a classroom or school newsletter, takes time that cuts into the already busy schedules of most school personnel. The implementation of a schoolwide program will require many hours to organize, implement, support, and evaluate the effectiveness. Simply put, school personnel who want to involve family and community members in their schools should expect to add to their already demanding workloads.

An additional concern related to involvement programs is the issue of sharing power. Inviting families to become actively involved requires that educators listen to their ideas and suggestions. Successful involvement programs are not one-way streets with volunteers simply carrying out orders from teachers and administrators. Volunteers will be more committed if their suggestions are sought and integrated into the program. Therefore, school personnel will need to establish effective lines of two-way communication and be willing to recognize and use the creative contributions of volunteers. Additionally, some parents and family members may want to become more involved in their child's education than is generally expected. Directing the enthusiasm of these parents to benefit the overall school program will require skills to channel concerns and ideas into the school's improvement plan. Again, school personnel must be willing to listen to and collaborate with family members, and invest the time required to welcome and sustain their involvement. In this way, the challenges associated with school involvement will become opportunities for school improvement.

CONCLUSION

Because family profiles and needs vary dramatically, a variety of involvement opportunities need to be in place to involve the families of all children. By broadening the scope of involvement opportunities, greater numbers of families will be able to participate in home–school partnerships and, therefore, contribute to the development and success of their children. Ongoing preparation and professional development of teachers and caregivers of children and adolescents is critical to the full involvement of families in their education and care.

APPLICATION
Working with Families

We have seen how important it is for family members to play an active role in the education of their children. However, most family members have jobs, housekeeping chores, bills to pay, groceries to buy, and dozens of other essential activities that demand their time. Families without jobs or homes are going to place even less of a priority on school-related issues. Teachers are members of families, too, and you may find the effort and thought required to encourage families of students to become involved to be overwhelming. Consider teaming with your colleagues in a more systematic approach to reach all parents in the school. If everyone in the school shares in the work, no individual teacher will be burdened.

For example, consider doing a monthly newsletter of student essays on "learning strategies" as a schoolwide project. Solicit the help of the high school journalism class or students in a local community college English class to coordinate and publish the articles written by students. Foreign-language classes could take on the challenge of translating the articles. Keep the articles short enough so the task doesn't become overly burdensome. Elementary and middle school teachers in each grade level could work with students on writing the essays as extensions of class discussions. High school teachers could do a similar project in English or social studies classes. Themes for the newsletter might include specific study skills, test taking strategies, improving reading comprehension, vocabulary development, and health tips for better learning.

As a regular feature in the newsletter, include a section on family members. Ask students to interview a family member about their school experiences asking questions similar to these: What was their favorite subject and why? What did they find difficult about learning when they were in school? What would have made it easier for them to learn? What have they done to help their own children succeed in school? The purpose of the interviews is not to come up with world-class journalistic features, but to encourage students and families to express their feelings about school.

Monitor the tone of the newsletters with your colleagues to keep the focus light and pleasant to read. If the children write about what they watch on television or why they like to visit the library, it will have more of an impact on parents than instructional statements from school administrators and teachers about how parents should monitor their children's television viewing or how critical it is to take their children to the library. Most families will enjoy seeing their child's work featured and hopefully they will gain insight into their own parenting skills. If work from all of the children is included as the year progresses, parents and family members will look forward to receiving the newsletters. The newsletter project also provides opportunities for parents to get involved in conversations with their children about school.

The case study that follows illustrates how a young single father who is trying to cooperate with his small son's school misses important communications from the teacher. His involvement as a parent is limited to helping his son with his homework assignments and dealing with problems that develop at school. The names of the characters have been changed, but the situation is based on an actual event. As a teacher, you are likely to encounter similar situations.

CASE STUDY: *Can't Rules be Bent?*
_____

It was nearly 6:00 P.M. It had been a long day for Patrick, a single parent, who had spent most of his working day hauling shingles to the roof of a housing complex. He enjoyed his roofing job, but hauling shingles up ladders, especially in hot weather, was strenuous and exhausting work. He was tired, and his back hurt. He thought of taking a long, hot soak in the bathtub and going to bed early to recoup his strength for the next day's work at the same building site. He knew, however, that it would be several hours before he could give in to such a temptation. His plans had to be worked around Sean, his 6-year-old son whom he had been raising by himself for the past 2 years, with occasional relief help from Sean's grandparents.

Sean continued to talk about the diorama he had to make and take to school the next day. Sean was excited about the project; in fact, he spoke of nothing else during the half-hour drive home from the Aftercare Center where he stayed every day after school until 5:15 P.M. when his dad picked him up after work.

"How long have you known about this project?" Patrick asked his son.

"Oh, Mrs. Bock told us about it last week, but I forgot. Lots of kids brought their boxes to school today, and they're really neat. I want mine to show a playground like the one in the Commons, you know? We can put lots of neat stuff in it, just like it is in the Commons. Will you help me, Daddy? I need a shoe box and colored paper, like green for grass and blue for sky, some branches for trees, dirt, and stuff like that. We can make the play things out of sticks and string and bottle caps and stuff like that. Mrs. Bock said that we need to use things from around the house. Can we do it now, Daddy? Do we have a shoe box?"

Patrick, with a slight smile, nodded and responded, "We'll work on it after we've eaten. Right now I've got to fix supper. While I'm doing that, you go outside to gather some twigs, dirt, and pebbles. And bring in the mail, too," he added.

As they sat down to eat, Patrick noticed the mail Sean had placed on the table. His attention was drawn to an envelope from Sean's school, which he opened immediately. The envelope contained a bill for $30.00 to cover the replacement cost of one "unreturned/lost" library book that had been checked out in Sean's name earlier that month. Written in bold letters at the bottom of the bill were the words, "Final Notice. Please pay immediately."

Naturally, Sean didn't know anything about the book, except that he "sorta remembered" getting a book from the library and "kinda thought" he had put it into his book bag to bring home. A search of the apartment failed to produce the missing book. An inquiring call to Sean's grandparents also failed to locate the book. At 10:00 P.M., the diorama project finished, Patrick shooed Sean to bed. Before retiring, Patrick set the alarm to wake up 15 minutes earlier than usual. His plan was to get Sean to school a little earlier the next morning so that he would have time to straighten out the library book issue and still get to work by eight o'clock.

At 7:30 the next morning, diorama and library book letter in hand, Patrick walked Sean to his classroom. Mrs. Bock was sitting at her desk. After greeting the two and admiring Sean's diorama, Mrs. Bock informed Sean that she would still give him "full credit" for the project even though it was late, but that in the future she would deduct points for late work.

Curious, Patrick asked about the assignment, indicating that he had heard no mention of the project until the previous evening. Patrick glanced around the room observing numerous dioramas on display as Mrs. Bock explained that Sean was probably reminded of the assignment yesterday when most of the children brought their completed dioramas to class. She added that the children had been given the assignment 3 weeks prior to yesterday's due date and had been reminded of the assignment several times over the past 3 weeks. In fact, she had highlighted the project and encouraged parents to help their children build their dioramas in this month's classroom newsletter that was sent home with the students last week.

Patrick informed Mrs. Bock that he never saw the newsletter, and apologized for Sean's being late with the project. Patrick then showed Mrs. Bock the $30.00 bill for the library book and asked for clarification. Mrs. Bock told Patrick that he would have to speak with Ms. Bind, the librarian, about the matter. She directed Patrick to the library and told Sean to wait in the cafeteria with the other children until the bell rang permitting them to go to their classrooms. Patrick gave Sean a hug, told him he'd pick him up at the Aftercare Center later that afternoon, and, conscious of the time, headed to the library.

Ms. Bind was adamant about the $30.00 bill. "It has to be paid," she said, "because it is school policy. I sent messages home with Sean on two occasions saying that the book needed to be returned. Mrs. Bock and I even looked in

Sean's classroom, his desk, and his book bag for that book. If it's not at home, then he must have lost it. And if it's lost, it must be replaced. The cost of replacing the book is $30.00. I'm sorry, sir," she continued, "but that's the way it is; it's school policy and only Mr. Sheets can make exceptions to this policy."

Patrick explained that he examined Sean's book bag nightly, and that he never saw any notices about the missing book, didn't know where the book was, and didn't have $30.00 to pay for it. In the background Patrick heard the bell releasing the children from the cafeteria. Suddenly, the hallways were filled with children scurrying to their classrooms. Patrick was aware that if he had to find and perhaps wait to speak to Mr. Sheets, he would be late for work. Showing his anxiety, he said to Ms. Bind somewhat sharply, "Look, I'm raising Sean by myself on a very fixed income, and $30.00 is a lot of money for me to come up with. Right now I have to be on my way to work; otherwise, I'll be late. I can't make phone calls from my work site, so would you ask Mr. Sheets to give me a call at home tonight to discuss the matter?"

CASE STUDY DISCUSSION GUIDE

Themes: Creating family-friendly school environments; quality of school-to-home communication practices; conflict between school policy and needs of nontraditional families.

Actors

A. How would you characterize each of the actors in this case? (List each person's name and give one-, two-, or three-word descriptors for each actor.)

Probes

1. How do you think each of the actors in this case feels?
2. Do you think of Patrick as being a parent who is involved in Sean's schooling? Why or why not?
3. How did Patrick feel about the school when he arrived? How did he feel when he left?
4. What kind of teacher do you suspect Mrs. Bock to be? How does she feel about Sean? What behaviors support your claims?
5. How does Ms. Bind feel about Sean? Patrick?

Issues

B. What are the major issues in this case? (Make a list of these issues.)

Probes

1. Did Ms. Bind treat Patrick's concern effectively?
2. What does Ms. Bind's behavior suggest about her role as a member of the school staff? What actions support your claim?
3. Is Sean's behavior typical for his age? Could Sean's behavior have been anticipated?

4. Is Patrick being unreasonable for not wanting to pay the $30.00 fine? Is he being unreasonable for insisting that Mr. Sheets phone him at home later that night?
5. Should exceptions to rules ever be made? Explain why or why not.
6. How could the school support Patrick in his role as a single parent?
7. To what extent are school personnel expected to bend school rules for individual students?
8. Should school personnel be held equally responsible for the learning achievement of all children regardless of their home backgrounds?

Problems or Conflicts

C. What are the major problems or conflicts in this case? Make a list of these problems or conflicts and specify whether you think they stem from personal or institutional origins. Now, examine the list further. Separate the items on your list into primary and secondary subcategories. (After completing this last step, you may find it easier to suggest solutions to the problems or conflicts in this case.)

Solutions

D. How could the problems in this case have been avoided? If you had been one of the actors in this case, what would you have done differently?

Probes

1. Was Sean's behavior predictable? Could it have been averted?
2. What could Patrick have done to become aware of Sean's homework assignment and the school's library policy?
3. What could Mrs. Bock have done to make sure Patrick knew of Sean's assignment?
4. What could Ms. Bind have done to ensure that Patrick knew of the missing library book and the consequences for not returning it?
5. Could a change in school policy have avoided the problems or conflicts experienced in this case? If so, what changes should be instituted?

SUPPLEMENTAL ACTIVITIES

The following activities include two types of field experiences: a school-based activity and a community-based activity. The school activity can be done as you complete your early field experiences that require observations at a school site. The community activity is designed to acquaint you with social service agencies that provide family support and resources. (Appendix C contains detailed directions for participant observations, and Appendix A contains suggested community resources.)

School-Based Activity

As you observe and participate in schools, look for behaviors, events, and activities that characterize family-friendly schools. You may want to focus your inquiries and observations on one or more of the following questions:

1. Does the office staff greet visitors in a friendly, courteous way?

2. Does the school provide an orientation program for families new to the school?

3. Do parents have access to teachers and administrators beyond the school day?

4. Are family members invited to make appointments with teachers to visit classrooms?

5. Does the school have a school-home-school communication system in place that includes methods of communicating with illiterate or limited-English-speaking families, and families with no telephones?

6. Does the school have an adequate communication system for informing all parents about school and classroom rules, school and classroom policies, parent–teacher conferences, and bus and lunch schedules?

7. Is there a resource center that provides parenting information for families and teachers?

8. Is there a bulletin board on which families can post news and announcements?

9. Is there a procedure for addressing family concerns about student placement and making adjustments when necessary?

10. What procedure is in place for parents to offer suggestions or ask questions about the school program?

Community-Based Activity

Interview the principal and the school guidance counselor (if there is one) to see what types of resources are available to parents in the community. Check the local phone directory to identify agencies that offer support to single parents. Call or visit these agencies to discuss their services and fee structure. You might want to prepare an annotated list of these resources to present to the school if one doesn't already exist. You may want to focus your inquiries and observations on one or more of the following questions:

1. Do any agencies offer mediation services to parents to help them solve school-related problems?

2. What types of child-care facilities are available in the neighborhood?

3. Do any agencies provide free or fee-based afterschool programs?

4. Do any agencies offer counseling in parenting skills?

As an alternative to using the **Case Study Discussion Guide,** you may want to reflect on the case and construct a written response to the following prompts:

1. Describe how you would have made certain that all parents were aware of the diorama homework assignment.

2. Describe a procedure for ensuring that all parents know school policies. Make sure your description accounts for the variety of family structures characteristic of contemporary families.

3. How would you describe a family-friendly school? Include characteristics of such a school in your response.

Participate in a role playing exercise. You may want to role play being a single parent raising a child (or children) with little assistance from family members or other characters portrayed in "Can't Rules be Bent?" As the roles are acted out, observers will want to take notes on their perceptions of the differences in parenting demands required of single-parent families versus two-parent families. Construct a list of these differences.

DISCUSSION

Form two groups and compare your lists. If there are not enough participants to make two groups, exchange ideas as one large group.

IMPLICATIONS FOR FAMILY INVOLVEMENT

Develop either individually or with your classmates a list of implications for family involvement applicable to both single-parent and two-parent families. You may want to modify your list after listening to the comments and insights of your peers.

REFERENCES

Ames, C., De Stefano, L., Watkins, T., & Sheldon, S. (1995). *Teachers' school-to-home communications and parent involvement: The role of parent perceptions and beliefs* (Report No. 28). Baltimore: Center on Families, Communities, Schools, and Children's Learning, Johns Hopkins University.

Barton, P. E., & Coley, R. J. (1992). *America's smallest school: The family.* Princeton, NJ: Educational Testing Service.

Booth, A., & Dunn, J. (Eds.). (1996). *Family-school links: How do they affect educational outcomes?* Mahwah, NJ: Erlbaum.

Center on Families, Communities, Schools, and Children's Learning (1994). *Parent involvement: The*

relationship between school-to-home communication and parents' perceptions and beliefs. Baltimore: Center on Families, Communities, Schools, and Children's Learning.

Christensen, C. M. (1992). Multicultural competencies in early intervention: Training professionals for a pluralistic society. *Infants and Young Children, 4,* 49–83.

Coleman, J. S., Campbell, E. Q., Hobson, C. J., McPartland, J., Mood, A. M., Weinfeld, F. D., et al. (1966). *Equality of educational opportunity.* Washington, DC: U.S. Government Printing Office.

Collins, T., Dewees, S., & Togneri, W. (1999). *School-community relations and contribution to student achievement.* Concept paper delivered to the Board of Directors of AEL, Inc., December 17, 1999, Lexington, KY.

Cooksey, E. C., & Fondell, M. M. (1996). Spending time with his kids: Effects of family structure on fathers' and children's lives. *Journal of Marriage and the Family, 58,* 693–707.

Epstein, J. L. (1995). School-family-community partnerships: Caring for the children we share. *Phi Delta Kappan, 76,* 701–712.

Epstein, J. L., Coates, L., Salinas, K. C., Sanders, M. G., & Simon, B. S. (1997). *School, family, and community partnerships: Your handbook for action.* Thousand Oaks, CA: Corwin Press.

Fan, X., & Chen, M. (1999). *Parental involvement and students' academic achievement: A meta-analysis.* Paper presented at the Annual Meeting of the American Educational Research Association. (ERIC Document Reproduction Service No. ED430048)

Henderson, A. T., & Berla, N. (1981). *The evidence grows: Parent involvement improves student achievement.* Columbia, MD: National Committee for Citizens in Education.

Henderson, A. T. (1987). *The evidence continues to grow: Parent involvement improves student achievement.* Columbia, MD: National Committee for Citizens in Education.

Henderson, A. T., & Berla, N. (1994). *A new generation of evidence: The family is critical to student achievement.* Columbia, MD: National Committee for Citizens in Education.

Hoover-Dempsey, K., & Sandler, H. (1995). Parental involvement in children's education: Why does it make a difference? *Teachers College Record, 97,* 310–331.

Hoover-Dempsey, K., & Sandler, H. (1997). Why do parents become involved in their children's education? *Review of Educational Research, 67,* 3–42.

Keith, T. Z., & Keith, P. B. (1993). Does parental involvement affect eighth-grade student achievement? Structural analysis of national data. *School Psychology Review, 22*(3), 474–496.

National PTA. (1998). *National standards for parent/family involvement programs.* Chicago: Author. Available from the national PTA Web site, http://www.pta.org/programs/invstand.htm

Nord, C. W., Brimhall, D., & West, J. (1997). *Fathers' involvement in their children's schools.* Washington, DC: U.S. Department of Education, National Center for Education Statistics.

Olmstead, P. P., & Rubin, R. I. (1983). Linking parent behaviors to child achievement: Four evaluation studies from the parent education follow-through program. *Studies in Educational Evaluation, 8,* 317–325.

Swick, K. (1984). *Inviting parents into the young child's world.* Champagne, IL: Stipes.

Swick, K., & Manning, L. (1983). Father involvement in home and school settings. *Childhood Education, 60,* 128–134.

Thomson, E., McLanahan, S. S., & Curtin, R. B. (1992). Family structure, gender, and parental socialization. *Journal of Marriage and the Family, 54*(2), 368–378.

U.S. Department of Education, National Center for Education Statistics. (1996). *National Household Education Survey of 1996: Data File User's Manual, 1* (NCES 97-425). Washington, DC: Author.

U.S. Department of Education. (1997). Fathers' involvement in their children's schools. Nord, C.W., Brimhall, D., & West, J. National Center for Education Statistics: Washington, D.C.

West, J., Denton, K., & Germino-Hausken, E. (2000, February). *America's kindergardners. Early childhood longitudinal study, kindergarten class of 1998–99.* Washington, DC: U.S. Government Printing Office, (GPO #065-000-01292-8)

3

UNDERSTANDING FAMILIES OF VARYING INCOME LEVELS

Poverty is the extent to which an individual does without resources.

—Ruby K. Payne,
A Framework for Understanding Poverty, 1998

ISSUES RELATED TO POVERTY

More than 12 million children live in poverty in the United States. Nearly one fourth of children under the age of 18 are poor (National Center for Children in Poverty [NCCP], 2003). What does it mean to live in poverty? What realities in the lives of children and their families are implied by this staggering statistic? Of extreme importance to educators is the question of how the realities of poverty affect children's school attendance and performance, and the involvement of their families in their education. Gaining an understanding of the realities of poverty is an essential first step in preparing teachers to serve the needs of students and their families who are poor.

UNDERSTANDING POVERTY

When is a family living in poverty? There are two measures of poverty established by the U.S. government: the U.S. Census Bureau and the U.S. Department of Health and Human Services (HHS). Poverty thresholds and guidelines are issued each year to determine the number of U.S. citizens living in poverty and their eligibility for federal assistance programs. The 2003 threshold for a family of four was $18,400. This threshold figure didn't enable a family to meet its basic needs; it merely allowed the family to exist marginally.

Families living in poverty do not have the resources to take care of basic needs (e.g., food, shelter, utilities, clothing, medical care, child care, and transportation). This means, of course, that neither do families living in poverty have the resources to pay for cars, health insurance, orthodontists, computers, vacations, designer clothes, or the many other goods and services available to families with higher income levels. For this reason, children of poverty often don't see themselves fitting in or belonging to mainstream society. When these children enter school lacking the social skills to integrate into the social structure of the school, they may experience bullying and other forms of aggressive behavior (Espelage, Bosworth, & Simon, 2000). Feelings and experiences of

Children and youth who live in poverty find it difficult to participate in school-sponsored social events due to their lack of material resources. How might their lack of participation influence their academic success?

alienation are likely to present serious challenges to teachers trying to integrate students and their families who are poor into the school community.

Living in poverty also means that families face a daily existence of stress and unpredictability. A harsher winter than usual, for example, may force a choice between paying a heating bill or buying food; and the loss of a job may easily result in homelessness. Certainly, when children fail to eat properly or receive adequate rest and sleep, their capacity to learn is significantly diminished. Poor children also lag behind other children academically and developmentally (Hack, Klein, & Taylor, 1995; Molnar, Rath, & Klein, 1991; Rafferty, 1991), causing them to need a variety of medical and support services that may be difficult to obtain, especially in rural areas. When caregivers are faced with surviving and providing for the most basic of needs, they are frequently unable to spend time with their children monitoring their behavior, talking and listening to them, or helping them participate in experiences that will develop learning skills necessary for school success. Single parents living in poverty have even less time to spend on such activities with their children.

Families living in poverty must also face the challenges of living in unattractive houses and neighborhoods frequently marked by violence and crime. There is strong evidence that aggressive behavior is more common among children and adolescents raised in lower socioeconomic neighborhoods than among their age-mates in middle-class settings (Atwater, 1992; Johnson & Friesen, 1993). Researchers attribute this aggressive behavior in large part to the fact that poor neighborhoods serve as training grounds for learning and sustaining aggressive habits (Bandura, 1991; Dodge, 1993). They also point to the parenting behaviors of caregivers in poverty households where aggressive behavior is commonly modeled (Dodge, Pettit, & Bates, 1994; Patterson, Reid, & Dishion, 1992). In these family settings, aggressive behavior is often used to solve conflicts, and children are encouraged to "stand up for themselves" by using physical force (Capaldi & Patterson, 1991).

Living in aggressive environments has been found to have a negative influence on children's social and educational adjustment (Sampson & Earls, 1995). Children living in poverty neighborhoods commonly attend schools where the student population is composed of individuals mainly from lower socioeconomic backgrounds. It is not surprising that the aggressive behaviors children and adolescents of poverty learn in their neighborhoods accompany them to school. Because the school culture punishes aggressive behavior, students from poor neighborhoods frequently find themselves further alienated from school and its learning opportunities. Working with children and families of poverty, therefore, presents a tremendous challenge to school personnel who must welcome and integrate them into the school while changing their social behavior to comply with school expectations.

Children and youth living in poverty environments may witness aggressive and violent behavior on a regular basis. How might these experiences influence student behavior at school?

(Family and community involvement programs that address the special needs of children and families of poverty are treated in Chapter 7.)

STEREOTYPING

A number of stereotypes exist about people living in poverty. Many believe that people who are poor are people of color who live in inner cities, are too lazy to work, and that they wouldn't be poor if they just worked harder. In reality, a majority of children of poverty in the United States are non-Hispanic Whites (Federal Interagency Forum on Child and Family Statistics, 1999). Although a number of children who live in inner cities are among the poor, some of the poorest families in the country live in rural areas. In fact, 535 U.S. counties that have consistently fallen below the poverty level in the past four census years have been classified as "Rural Persistent Poverty" counties by the U.S. Department of Agriculture (Carter, 1999). Additionally, there is no empirical evidence that people of poverty are too lazy to work. Rather, there are sound socioeconomic causes of poverty in the United States. Among these causes is the elimination of many blue-collar jobs, the increased percentage of children living in single-mother families, and the decline in government benefits (Anderson, Janger, & Panton, 1995; Huston, McLoyd, & McColl, 1994). In fact, two thirds of all young children who are poor live in families with at least one employed parent (NCCP, 2003). These families are classified by the Census Bureau as "working poor."

Parents working in minimum wage jobs may not attend school functions. These parents could easily be judged as being disinterested in their child's schooling, when in reality, to attend school functions may require taking off from work and losing income. How might school personnel involve these parents?

It is not uncommon for teachers to maintain a deficit view of low-income families, believing that low-income parents fail to value education or have little to offer to the education of their children (Davies, 1988, 1991; Finders & Lewis, 1994). Teachers may be tempted to interpret the absence of low-income parents in school activities to mean the families are not interested in their children's education. In reality, they care about their children as much as other parents do, but circumstances prevent them from becoming involved. If they are employed at low-level jobs, they may not be able to miss work without also missing pay. Other factors preventing parental involvement among poor families are the parents' lack of education and limited knowledge of the education system. Fuller and Tutwiler (1998) point out that substantial numbers of parents living in poverty dropped out of school before receiving a high school diploma. Additionally, immigrant parents, although they care about their children's education, may have limited involvement with their children's school because they feel intimidated by their lack of knowledge of the school culture (Stronge & Popp, n.d.).

HOMELESSNESS

Whereas all children living in poverty suffer from a lack of resources, children who are homeless face even greater barriers. Even though the law allows homeless children to remain at the school they attended prior to becoming homeless, many are unable to do so because homeless shelters may be located a great distance from the home school. Also, circumstances may force homeless children to be moved from shelter to shelter, resulting in numerous changes in schools along with repeated episodes of dealing with guardianship, immunization requirements, and gaps in curricula. Children who are homeless also experience added stress because they have lost their sense of place. They miss their pets, their friends, their clothes, and their possessions. In many instances they are stigmatized by their homelessness and ridiculed by their new classmates (Reed-Victor & Pelco, 1999).

How widespread is the problem of homelessness among children? Rafferty and Shinn (1991) noted that the "economic decline" of the 1980s generated an unprecedented rise in the number of homeless families with children in the United States. The trend continues today with homeless children constituting the fastest-growing segment of the homeless population (National Coalition for the Homeless, 1998). The average homeless parent is a young single mother with one or two children. She reads at or below the 6th-grade level and left school by the 10th grade (Nunez & Collignon, 1997). These young parents may be unable to provide a stable environment for their children while living as a homeless family.

Children whose families are homeless may not reveal their situations to their teachers or to the school administration. Parents may not reveal this information either because they may be embarrassed about their living situation, worried that their children will be ridiculed, or afraid that they could lose their children to protective services.

Homeless children and youth face significant barriers that have a negative impact on their success in school. It is not uncommon for homeless students to be enrolled in several schools during the same academic year.

Teachers should approach all families with sensitivity and respect; however, even more care is needed when children are from homeless families. Homeless parents are as concerned about their children's progress in school as other parents and can become viable partners in education with encouragement and support (Stronge & Hudson, 1999).

SCHOOL PRACTICES THAT DIFFERENTIATE

Children bring the effects of poverty with them to school. They can't pay for field trips, school projects, school pictures, or special materials. They may not be able to participate in school sports because they lack the money to keep pace with the activities of other team members. In many instances, not having the resources to wear clothing like their classmates may cause children to avoid school altogether. School personnel unknowingly exclude many poor children and families from participating in important aspects of the school program by scheduling conferences and other school events on a once-only basis, thus limiting the participation of parents who have limited transportation or child-care options. Teachers can show their respect for families living in poverty by scheduling meetings at times and places convenient to them.

UPPER SOCIO-ECONOMIC FAMILIES

At the opposite end of the socioeconomic scale are the families who are well educated and financially comfortable. They have the resources to provide for basic needs (e.g., food, shelter, utilities, clothing, medical care, child care, and transportation), as well as advantages such as health insurance, orthodontists, designer clothes, vacations, and home computers. They are able to provide a stimulating environment that is highly verbal and technologically rich with age-appropriate books, toys, and games. They encourage their children to explore different environments. They are able to take them to museums and other educationally enriching sites. Numerous correlational studies indicate that richer home environments and experiences are associated with more advanced cognitive, linguistic, and academic development in children (Brooks-Gunn, Klebanov, & Duncan, 1996; Hart & Risley, 1995; Jimerson, Egeland, & Teo, 1999).

Families in upper socioeconomic situations often are highly involved in their children's schools because they have the resources that allow them to take time off from work to attend school activities. They also tend to have reached higher levels of academic achievement and are comfortable in the school environment. These families place greater demands on schools and hold teachers accountable for meeting their children's learning needs. Teachers need to be aware of the intense interest of these parents to become involved in school curricula decisions, classroom activities, and their children's learning. Their enthusiasm for becoming involved can often be channeled into positive activities that support the teacher.

CONCLUSION

Because of their vulnerability and wide range of support needs, teachers and administrators should exercise the utmost understanding and respect for children and families of poverty. Regardless of a family's socioeconomic status, parents remain the first and foremost teachers of their children. All families have vast opportunities to influence their children by instruction and example. All parents want their children to do well in school and live lives of quality. If they are given appropriate support and opportunity, all parents will work with school personnel to help their children learn. By working together, families and schools can make a significant difference in the lives of countless children victimized by poverty.

APPLICATION
Working with Families

Students from families with limited financial resources find it difficult to participate in many extracurricular activities. As students enter the upper grades, it becomes even more important to them to be like their peer group. They want to dress like other students and be part of the total school program. Many schools and community agencies have established a pool of funds to help students who are not able to afford field trips, school pictures, yearbooks, or special equipment for extracurricular activities.

Students who need financial assistance to participate in school activities probably will be too embarrassed to ask for help. They may make up excuses for not participating; or if they are old enough, they may drop out of school. Teachers can play a key role in identifying students who may need help. Observe students to see if there are any who may not be getting adequate food, rest, or health care. Students in these situations may appear to be easily distracted, unable to focus, restless or sleepy, poorly groomed, and perhaps have an offensive body odor.

Schools and community organizations can partner in helping these students. Schools can make arrangements for students to take a shower at school and wash their clothes. Parent organizations can maintain thrift shops housed in the school to provide clothing to students at little or no cost. School staff should make sure that all families are aware of free or reduced price breakfast and lunch programs. Information about these programs and other resources can be distributed in notices posted in community grocery stores and laundromats, by public service announcements on local radio stations; and, for parents who don't speak English, telephone calls from other parents who can speak their language.

Students who participate in these government programs should not be labeled or publicly identified. Schools should develop a system for collecting vouchers in the school lunchroom that doesn't stigmatize students who are receiving free or reduced price breakfasts or lunches. Teachers should review how they are assigning homework to make sure students aren't required to use resources that may not be available to them. Are students being asked to use computers at home, visit the library, use an encyclopedia, or build models out of special materials?

School fundraisers present additional problems for students from low-income families. When schools undertake fundraising drives that pit one classroom against another to sell the most candy bars or Christmas wrap, students with limited resources may feel disassociated from classmates when they can't afford to buy items or their families can't participate. Schools should offer options for students who might not be able to participate in fundraising avenues.

Teachers should rotate members of collaborative working groups and student teams to prevent particular students from always being excluded or chosen last. It is not uncommon for students who are different from their peers to be ridiculed and teased. These and other forms of bullying behavior have a critical negative impact on the entire learning community. Schools should have strategies for stopping bullying behavior and clear procedures for dealing with both offenders and victims. All school personnel should be quick to enforce school policy regarding bullying behavior.

The following case study illustrates how a young girl feels isolated and different from her classmates because of her family's socioeconomic status. She is a target of ridicule from her peers because of her physical appearance and lack of resources. The names of the characters have been changed, but the situation is based on an actual event. As a teacher, you are likely to encounter similar situations.

CASE STUDY: *Is Anyone Listening?*

Jenny sat in her seventh-grade English class staring at the blank sheet of paper on the desk in front of her. She fingered her pencil aimlessly. From time to time she glanced at the words on the board that Mr. Matty had written as a writing prompt: "I am (your name), and this is what is special about me." She knew what Mr. Matty was doing: He was trying to get to know his new seventh-grade students and find out how good they were at writing and spelling. "Yeah, like he really cares about me," thought Jenny. "He's probably like all the other teachers who like the good students who are popular and who come from nice homes. Well, that leaves me out on all counts." As Jenny continued fingering her pencil, she thought of what she was tempted to write: "Take a good look at me Mr. Matty, you can't miss me! I'm in the seventh grade and I weigh 200 pounds. Yeah, I'm in the seventh grade and I can only read third-grade books; and I can't write much better. That's why I'm sitting in the last seat back here by the door where nobody can see me. This way, maybe they won't tease me so much. They've teased me in the past, over and over again. I hate it when they call me Dumbo and sniff the air when they pass me. And they never ask me to join them for anything. God, how I hate school. I wish I wasn't here. And, I won't go to PE class either. I hate wearing those dumb shorts they make you wear; and the ones I got today are too small. But the teacher said they're the biggest ones he has. Well, I ain't wearin' 'em, 'cause the kids will just laugh at me again. So, who am I? I'm Jenny Schmidt. I weigh 200 pounds and everybody hates me. My mom don't even care about me. She's always makin' me watch the little kids while she runs around with her friends. I wish she had a job. We never go places or do things. The TV's broke too, and I only have one pair of jeans."

CASE STUDY DISCUSSION GUIDE

Themes: The school's degree of involvement in a student's life; dealing with social services; teacher insensitivity; availability of school remedial and other support programs; teasing and bullying at school.

Actors

A. How would you characterize each of the actors in this case? (List each person's name and give one-, two-, or three-word descriptions for each actor.)

Probes

1. How do you think each of the actors in this case feels?
2. What kind of teacher is Mr. Matty?
3. What kind of teacher is the PE teacher?
4. What kind of mother is Jenny's mom?

Issues

B. What are the major issues in this case? (Make a list of these issues.)

Probes

1. Do you believe the adults are acting responsibly? Why or why not?
2. Do you believe Jenny is acting responsibly? Why or why not?
3. Who is responsible for Jenny? How?
4. Why does Jenny say "everybody hates me"?

5. Is Jenny justified in her claim? Is she overreacting?
6. Is Jenny able to see herself (and others) differently at this time? Why or why not?
7. Is Jenny giving a reasonable account of Mr. Matty's intentions?
8. Is Jenny being unreasonable in her expectations?
9. Do you think Mr. Matty's writing exercise is a good one? Why or why not?
10. Should all students in a class be given the same assignment?
11. Should some writing topics be considered "off limits"?
12. What criteria should be used when selecting writing topics?

Problems or Conflicts

What are the problems or conflicts in this case? Make a list of these problems or conflicts and specify whether you think they stem from personal or institutional origins. Now, examine the list further. Can you separate the items on your list into primary and secondary subcategories? (After completing this last step, you may find it easier to suggest solutions to the problems or conflicts in this case.)

Solutions

How could the problems in this case have been avoided? If you had been one of the actors in this case, what would you have done differently?

Probes

1. What can school personnel do to help Jenny?
2. What could Jenny's mother do to help her?
3. What can Jenny do to help herself?
4. Should community services become involved in this case? If so, which services?
5. How could the problems in this case have been avoided?

SUPPLEMENTAL ACTIVITIES

The following activities include two types of field experiences: a school-based activity and a community-based activity. The school activity can be done as you complete your early field experiences that require observations at a school site. The community activity is designed to acquaint you with social service agencies that provide family support and resources. Detailed directions for participant observations during early field experiences are provided in Appendix C.

FIELD EXPERIENCE A   ***School-Based Activity***

As you observe and participate in schools, find out what the school's policy is for dealing with bully behavior. To what extent do school officials involve the parents of both bullies and bullied students to resolve and prevent future bully abuse? More generally, ask how the school provides for the physical and psychological comfort and safety of students while they are at school, both inside and outside the classroom, and to and from school.

Community-Based Activity

Inquire about community and social services that provide professional resources to students and their families when their needs cannot be met at school. Visit local social service offices to learn about the array of services they provide to students and families in need. Interview a social worker to learn more about what resources are most commonly needed in the region and ask for his or her perspective on how teachers can partner with social workers to be more effective in helping students.

As an alternative to using the **Case Study Discussion Guide,** you may want to reflect on the case and construct a written response to the following prompts:

1. How much "care" are teachers expected to give students?

2. To what extent are teachers expected to interfere in the child-rearing practices of parents?

3. Describe an event you are aware of in which a teacher was able to help a student by working with that child's family or a community agency.

You may want to role play a scenario in which a student is being bullied because of his or her socioeconomic status. One of your peers can play the part of a school official who becomes aware of the bullying activity. Actors may assume the characters portrayed in "Is Anyone Listening?" to begin the role playing. As the roles are acted out, observe how the school official deals with both students.

DISCUSSION

Construct a list of the official's intervention behavior as it was played out. Suggest how school officials might deal with students in this or a similar scenario.

IMPLICATIONS OF FAMILY INVOLVEMENT

Beyond dealing with the students involved in the bullying role play, did the school official take measures to involve the parents or families of the two students? Generate a list of ways to involve the families of both the bully and the bullied student in working with school personnel to help both students.

REFERENCES

Anderson, L. M., Janger, M. L., & Panton, K. L. (1995). *An evaluation of state and local efforts to serve the educational needs of homeless children and youth.* Washington, DC: Policy Studies Associates.

Atwater, E. (1992). *Adolescence* (2nd ed.). Upper Saddle River, NJ: Prentice Hall.

Bandura, A. (1991). Social-cognitive theory of moral thought and action. In W. M. Kurtines & J. L.

Gewirtz (Eds.), *Handbook of moral behavior and development: Vol. 1: Theory.* Hillsdale, NJ: Erlbaum.

Brooks-Gunn, J., Klebanov, P. K., & Duncan, G. J. (1996). Ethnic differences in children's intelligence test scores: Role of economic deprivation, home environment, and maternal characteristics. *Child Development, 67,* 396–408.

Capaldi, D. M., & Patterson, G. R. (1991). Relation of parental transitions to boys' adjustment problems: I. A linear hypothesis, II. Mothers at risk for transition and unskilled parenting. *Developmental Psychology, 27,* 489–504.

Carter, C. (1999, December). *Education and development in poor rural communities: An interdisciplinary research agenda.* Charleston, WV: ERIC Clearinghouse on Rural Education and Small Schools. (ERIC Document Reproduction Service No. ED438154)

Davies, D. (1988). Benefits of and barriers to parent involvement. *Community Education Research Digest, 2*(2), 1988.

Davies, D. (1991, January). Schools reaching out: Families, school, and community. *Phi Delta Kappan, 75*(5), 376–382.

Dodge, K. A. (1993). Social-cognitive mechanisms in the development of conduct disorder and depression. *Annual Review of Psychology, 44,* 59–584.

Dodge, K. A., Pettit, G. S., & Bates, J. E. (1994). Socialization mediation of the relation between socioeconomic status and child conduct problems. *Child Development, 65,* 649–665.

Espelage, D., Bosworth, K., & Simon, T. (2000). Examining the social context of bullying behaviors in early adolescence. *Journal of Counseling and Development, 78,* 326–333.

Federal Interagency Forum on Child and Family Statistics. (1999). *America's children: Key national indicators of well-being.* Washington, DC: U.S. Government Printing Office.

Finders, M., & Lewis, C. (1994). Why some parents don't come to school. *Educational Leadership, 5*(8), 50–54.

Fuller, M. L., & Tutwiler, S. D. (1998). Poverty: The enemy of children and families. In M. L. Fuller & G. Olsen (Eds.), *Home-school relations: Working successfully with parents and families.* Boston: Allyn & Bacon.

Hack, M., Klein, N., & Taylor, G. (1995). Long-term developmental outcomes of low birth weight infants. *The Future of Children, 5,* 176–196.

Hart, B., & Risley, T. R. (1995). *Meaningful differences in the everyday experiences of young American children.* Baltimore: Brookes.

Huston, A. C., McLoyd, V. C., & McColl, C. G. (1994). Children and poverty: Issues in contemporary research. *Child Development, 65,* 275–282.

Jimerson, S., Egeland, B., & Teo, A. (1999). A longitudinal study of achievement trajectories: Factors associated with change. *Journal of Educational Psychology, 91,* 116–126.

Johnson, H. C., & Friesen, B. (1993). Etiologies of mental and emotional disorders in children. In H. Johnson (Ed.), *Child mental health in the 1990s: Curricula for graduate and undergraduate.* Washington, DC: U.S. Department of Health and Human Services.

Molnar, J. M., Rath, W. R., & Klein, T. P. (1991). *Ill fares the land: The consequences of homelessness and chronic poverty for children and families in New York City.* New York: Bank Street College.

National Center for Children in Poverty. Retrieved September 30, 2003, from http://www.nccp.org/pub_lat.html

National Coalition for the Homeless. (1998). *Education of homeless children and youth* (Fact Sheet #10). Washington, DC: Author.

Nunez, R. Da Costa, & Collignon, K. (1997). Creating a community of learning for homeless children. *Educational Leadership, 55*(2), 56–60.

Patterson, G. R., Reid, J. B., & Dishion, T. J. (1992). *Antisocial boys.* Eugene, OR: Castalia.

Rafferty, Y. (1991). Developmental and educational consequences of homelessness on children and youth. In J. Kryder-Coe, L. Salamon, & J. Molnar (Eds.), *Homeless children and youth: A new American dilemma.* New Brunswick, NJ: Transaction Books.

Rafferty, Y., & Shinn, M. (1991). The impact of homelessness on children. *American Psychologist, 46*(11), 1170–1179.

Reed-Victor, D., & Pelco, L. (1999). Helping homeless students build resilience: What the school community can do. *Journal for a Just and Caring Education, 5*; 51–71.

Sampson, R. J., & Earls, F. (1995, April). *Community social organization in the urban mosaic: Project on human development in Chicago neighborhoods.* Paper presented at the meeting of the Society for Research. Chicago, Illinois.

Stronge, J. H., & Hudson, K. S. (1999). Educating homeless children and youth with dignity and care. *Journal for a Just and Caring Education, 5*(1), 7–18.

Stronge, J. H., & Popp, P. (Eds.). (n.d.). *The education of homeless children and youth: A compendium of research and information.* Greensboro, North Carolina: The Regional Educational Laboratory at SERVE.

U.S. Census Bureau. (2002, January 22). Retrieved February 14, 2002, from http://www.census.gov/hhes/www/poverty.html

U.S. Department of Health and Human Services. (2002, February 14). Retrieved February 17, 2002, from http://aspe/hhs.gov/poverty/poverty.html

UNDERSTANDING FAMILIES FROM DIFFERENT CULTURES

I know that good and caring teachers come in all colors and from all ethnic backgrounds. But, you know, I'm a history teacher, and I know that the misunderstanding spawned by racial, ethnic, and cultural differences can poison human relations. They can make it impossible for people to trust one another or to work together.

—Robert Chase, president, National Education Association, National Press Club Luncheon, Friday, November 16, 2001. Reprinted with permission of Federal News Service.

CULTURAL NORMS, CONFLICTS, AND NEEDS

The above remarks by Robert Chase direct attention to a basic issue that must be confronted by anyone preparing to work with students and families from cultures different from their own: How can cultural ignorance and misunderstanding be replaced with cultural awareness and appreciation resulting in the establishment of trusting cooperative relationships? This chapter explores what teachers must know and do to accommodate the learning needs of all children, and how the culturally driven norms for learning affect home–school communication. Specifically, we will look at racial and ethnic minorities as well as families living in rural areas whose culture is shaped by geographic location.

When we speak of understanding different cultures, we refer to the "many different factors that shape one's sense of group identity: race, ethnicity, religion, geographical location, income status, gender, and occupations" (Turnbull, Turnbull, Shank, & Leal, 1995). This cultural identity also directs the group's values, beliefs, ideologies, and rules of conduct (Mackelprang & Salsgiver, 1999). All of these factors combined have an impact on the nature and quality of social and learning relationships. Knowing how to work effectively with students from diverse cultures requires a familiarity with the ideas, values, and practices of the cultural groups that have shaped students' behavior and attitudes toward learning.

This knowledge is critical to the future success of public education in America because demographers predict that by the year 2010, 45% of the student population in U.S. public schools will consist of racial and ethnic minorities (Meece, 2002). Similarly, more students are expected to come from rural areas during the next decade. On the other hand, 95% of the current teaching force is from the White majority culture (Henry, 1990). Even more disturbing is the fact that individuals entering the teaching profession tend to come from mostly homogeneous backgrounds with little experience in diverse cultures (Ladson-Billings, 1999).

When teachers come from cultural backgrounds different from those of their students, they may easily misinterpret students' culturally based behavior as the basis for a referral to special education or a need for disciplinary action (Foster, 1986; Hanna, 1988). Students who display behaviors with which teachers are unfamiliar, especially those of recent immigrants (Sugai, 1988), are particularly susceptible to diagnosis for behavior disorders (Hanna, 1988; Sugai & Maheady, 1988). Teachers need to know about the differences in cultural styles of interaction to avoid misjudging students' intentions, abilities, and competencies in the classroom (Young & Edwards, 1996). Other problems arise when teachers use culturally inappropriate strategies and techniques to assist student learning (D'Andrea & Daniels, 1997; Mason, 1999; Sue & Sue, 1990). Teacher–parent communication and teacher–student communication can be blocked when culturally related linguistic and communication styles differ from mainstream expectations for "appropriate participation" (Eisenhart & Cutts-Dougherty, 1991; Franklin 1992). Without this knowledge, teachers may distance themselves from those they intend to serve.

The greatest learning strength students bring to school is their home and cultural experience. How can teachers build upon the learning strengths of students of different cultures?

To accommodate the needs of students and families from different cultures, the culture of the school itself must foster cultural pluralism, a concept reflecting the school's acceptance and celebration of cultural differences and its efforts to foster and encourage those differences (Turnbull et al., 1995). In the culturally responsive classroom, teachers organize instructional activities and performance expectations that accommodate the cultural practices, interests, and cognitive learning styles of minority students, including patterns of teacher–student and peer group interactions that enable academic achievement (Au & Kawakami, 1985; Au & Mason, 1983; Moore, 1996; Tharp & Gallimore, 1988).

EXPECTATIONS FOR CLASSROOM PARTICIPATION AND DEMONSTRATIONS OF COMPETENCE

It is important to avoid stereotypes when generalizing about the learning characteristics of specific racial and ethnic groups. The cultural norms and expectations for classroom behavior discussed in the following pages may not be displayed by all students who share the same social or ethnic background because they may have assimilated into the mainstream culture (Dunn & Griggs, 1996). It is important for teachers to understand that children are raised differently from one family to another, and that they need to identify the learning behaviors of individual students rather than start their relationship with a student on what may be false assumptions. However, the following generalizations may give teachers a better understanding of the relationship between culture and school success and, therefore, better enable them to organize culturally appropriate learning opportunities.

Students participate in learning through classroom social structures. Minority students are at a disadvantage when those social structures are incongruent with their cultural learning styles (Eisenhart & Cutts-Dougherty, 1991; Irvine & York, 1995). The incongruity between the learning styles of minority students and traditional mainstream classroom practice has been explained in large part by the linear step-by-step approach to learning that is characteristic of mainstream school curricula (Martel, 1998). This approach requires students to demonstrate social and learning strengths that reflect White middle-class cultural values, beliefs, and norms (Ogbu, 1988). For example, students attending mainstream schools are expected to use standard English, and to gain permission to speak rather than "blurt out" when answering questions or initiating interactions. Mainstream schools also expect students to follow conventional rules governing the appropriate use of body language during school. These rules include maintaining eye contact and standing "straight and tall" when interacting with authority figures, limiting body movement, and avoiding physical contact. The culture of mainstream schools also emphasizes the importance of competition among students and individual achievement (Bellah, Madsen, Sullivan, Swidler, & Tipton, 1985). Consequently, most mainstream schools also reflect the high value parents place on expecting preschool and kindergarten programs to teach children the basic academic skills that White middle-class students will need to succeed in school (Charlesworth, 1996; Dunn & Kontos, 1997; Elkind, 1988;

Roopnarine & Johnson, 2000). To this end, students attending mainstream schools are usually required to demonstrate learning achievement by successful performance on "paper-and-pencil" measures. These expectations for teaching and learning in mainstream schools are congruent with the learning expectations of students who espouse White middle-class values, but they are often in conflict with the social structure and cultural learning styles of many students from minorities.

CULTURAL AND SOCIAL STRUCTURES OF MINORITY GROUPS

This section illustrates the differences in cultural learning styles of five ethnic groups: African Americans, Arab Americans, Asian Americans, Mexican Americans, and Native Americans.

AFRICAN AMERICAN STUDENTS

African American students have a rich cultural heritage that places value on oral and kinesthetic learning, and prefers a focus on people rather than things. The learning environment that seems to foster academic success for African American students includes (1) flexible classroom environments, (2) frequent opportunities for teacher–student interaction, (3) field experiences, (4) small-group activities that encourage discussions with peers, and (5) cooperative learning tasks (Gilbert & Gay, 1983; Irvine & York, 1995). Obviously, all students could benefit from this type of learning environment.

Traditional values and stylistic differences in verbal and nonverbal communication common among African American students may include a lack of eye contact during interaction with an adult. In mainstream American culture, a child is expected to look at the authority figure when being addressed. Lowered eyes are associated with deceit or inattention (Kim, Shin, & Cai, 1998; Srebalus & Brown, 2001). To gain eye contact, the teacher may lift the student's chin and say "Look at me when I'm talking to you." The culturally uninformed teacher fails to realize that in many African American homes, children are taught to lower their eyes when being disciplined as a sign of respect and submission (Kim et al., 1998; Srebalus & Brown, 2001). Furthermore, direct eye contact by these students during disciplinary situations typically indicates defiance rather than respect (Hanna, 1988).

Many African American students communicate through body language with frequent head nods, blurting out, hand gestures, and changes in body position. They may speak in louder tones than other cultural groups. African American students are tolerant of physical closeness during interaction. Also, African American students are willing to share personal information as a sign of comraderie. (Gay, 1995; Srebalus & Brown, 2001). Teachers who are unfamiliar with the communication styles of African American students may complain that they are "noisy," "rambunctious," or even "rude." Many teachers view these behaviors as violations of proper classroom conduct and interruptions of their teaching (Eisenhart & Cutts-Dougherty, 1991; Irvine & York, 1995).

ARAB AMERICAN STUDENTS

Arab American students share many similarities with other immigrant groups seeking to establish an ethnic identity in a heterogeneous country. But they also face additional challenges resulting from negative stereotyping, discrimination, and widespread misinformation about their history and culture. For example, not all people in the Middle East are Arab (e.g., Iranians and Israelis) and not all Arabs are Muslim. Those Arab students who are Muslim must find ways to practice their religion in a predominantly Judeo-Christian country (Jackson, 1995).

Schools can eliminate some sources of cultural conflict by being sensitive to Muslim students' religious practices (Suleiman, 1996). Coed physical education classes, showering requirements, and brief sports uniforms are inconsistent with Muslim traditions of modesty. Girls who wear head coverings for religious reasons should be protected from ridicule. During the holy month of Ramadan, Muslim students of high school age fast from sunrise to sunset. Schools could permit students to go to the library instead of the cafeteria during Ramadan. (Council on American-Islamic Relations, 1997).

In the Arab culture, "saving face" is a valued norm. Students are uncomfortable in competitive learning environments because the unsuccessful student will be embarrassed before his peers. Traditional methods of promoting positive classroom behavior in American classrooms incorporate competitive situations that provide rewards of checks, gold stars, or prizes. This cultural learning approach may create problems for Arab American students who have attended school in their home country where noncompetitive learning environments are the norm.

Traditionally, education systems in the Middle East have depended heavily on rote memorization. Teachers often lecture while students take notes, memorize the content, and repeat it on examinations. This system discourages reasoning, analysis, and critical thinking. Students are not encouraged to ask questions or interrupt the teacher (Sluglett, 2002). In helping Arab American students to adapt to the American system, teachers should use cooperative, highly structured learning activities, encourage student questions, and model critical thinking.

Traditional values and stylistic differences in verbal and nonverbal communication common to African American students also can be found among Arab American students who avoid eye contact during interaction with adults because they have been taught that it is disrespectful (Sluglett, 2002). Like African American students, Arab American students are tolerant of physical closeness during interaction and tend to stand much closer during conversations than American students do.

The Arab culture places a high value on maintaining family privacy. Therefore, students may avoid disclosing information about personal or family concerns because of loyalty to the family.

Arab American students who are Muslim are believers in fatalism and attribute everything that happens to God's will. If they fail a test, even though it may have been because they didn't study, they may attribute it to "God's will." Although it is important to respect students' cultural beliefs, teachers also must help students understand their role in accepting responsibility for meeting academic standards and learning.

ASIAN AMERICAN STUDENTS

Asian American students reflect a traditional cultural heritage that believes in working for the benefit of the entire group, rather than competing with peers. Teachers can take advantage of this learning preference by having students work in small, cooperative learning groups. Teachers should avoid excessive individual public recognition of Asian American students because they may interpret these events as a violation of cultural expectations. Similarly, teachers can expect traditional Asian American students to be reluctant to volunteer answers during whole-group instructional settings or to speak of their own accomplishments. Many Asian American students are committed to achieving academic excellence, which they view as a tribute to their parents and family. Asian American students tend to be uncomfortable with public displays of emotion, which may be viewed as a sign of weakness and a betrayal of personal and family dignity.

Traditional values and stylistic differences in verbal and nonverbal communication common among Asian American students may include avoidance of direct eye contact during interactions, especially in the presence of authority figures, because it is viewed as a sign of disrespect. Asian American students may fold their arms across the chest as a sign of respect and reverence. Unfortunately, teachers may interpret this behavior as an indication that the student is bored or challenging their authority. Personal matters that embarrass or cause

Some cultures expect individuals to demonstrate their achievements within a group context. Individual recognition is frowned upon. What implications do such cultural expectations have for teachers?

hurt feelings or stress are usually discussed only with family members or very close friends. Asian American students respect physical distance during interactions and avoid physical contact, especially touching the head, because the body is regarded as a sacred edifice (Leung, 1988; Srebalus & Brown, 2001; Yee, 1988).

MEXICAN AMERICAN STUDENTS

Mexican American students, like Arab American and Asian American students, are loyal to group rather than individual achievement; therefore, they prefer a noncompetitive, highly structured learning environment based on group cooperation. Mexican American students tend to prefer kinesthetic learning activities that allow for experiential, hands-on participation. To meet the needs of Mexican American students, teachers are encouraged to use cooperative learning activities, humor, drama, fantasy, and modeling (Dunn & Griggs, 1996; Ramirez & Castaneda, 1974).

During classroom communication, Mexican American students tend to avoid direct eye contact with authority figures because in their culture it is a sign of intimacy. Teachers may interpret this behavior as a sign of disrespect or deceit because the mainstream culture expects eye contact to establish respect and credibility during interactions. A number of behaviors can lead teachers to conclude that their Mexican American students lack interest or enthusiasm. For example, Latin American students initially may be reserved and quiet. They may avoid self-disclosure to guard personal and family privacy. Mexican American students often avoid interrupting the teacher to ask a clarifying question because they consider it disrespectful to interrupt authority figures. During classroom interactions, the girls may behave passively because it is considered a more masculine trait to express opinions and display strong personalities (Srebalus & Brown, 2001).

NATIVE AMERICAN STUDENTS

There are more than 400 Native American tribes in the United States and they each have their own unique culture. However, Native Americans share common cultural characteristics pertaining to learning and communication. Teachers of Native American students are encouraged to organize students into small cooperative learning groups, to provide hands-on learning tasks, to present content by demonstration, to avoid individual achievement expectations, competition, giving lengthy directions, and extensive lecturing (Irvine & York, 1995; Sawyer, 1991).

Traditional values and stylistic differences in verbal and nonverbal communication common among Native American students may include a high regard for maintaining self-control in public and a loyalty to group achievement. Like the cultural groups discussed previously, Native Americans view direct eye contact as disrespectful. They may avoid nodding their heads or smiling because such behaviors represent public displays of emotion. They may avoid self-disclosure because it is seen as a loss of control. In the classroom they may avoid interrupting the teacher to show respect for authority (Srebalus & Brown, 2001).

Nearly half of the public schools in the United States are considered to be in rural areas and small towns, employing about 40% of the nation's public school teachers (National Education Association, 1998). Schools in communities with a population of 2,500 or less "enroll at least 20% of the K–12 students in the country" (Lewis, 2003). Working with students and families living in rural areas presents unique challenges because of the beliefs, values, expectations, and practices common to rural communities. The following suggestions will provide helpful direction for understanding and relating to students and families in rural settings (Diss, 2001).

In most rural communities the school is the center of social activity. Teachers need to view the school as more than a "place to work"; rather, it should be viewed as a place to establish community connections, to make friends, and to nurture community relationships. Teachers in rural schools can benefit from what community members have to say about the community, its beliefs, talents, community contributions, and needs. Learning about the histories of communities will help teachers to value the experiences of the community, its problems and struggles, its strengths and accomplishments. This knowledge will enable teachers to validate and celebrate the rich heritage of community members and their rural culture. For example, teachers in rural communities will find that parents want their children to graduate from high school, but believe that higher education takes young people away from the community. An underlying fear, and often a reality, is that the young person going away to college may not come back because of the limited economic opportunities in the rural community. Teachers in rural schools need to respect this belief system while helping students to value learning as a way to gain access to opportunity.

Many rural communities value education, but they also are committed to culturally imbedded activities that are in conflict with school activities. For example, large groups of students may be absent from school during hunting and harvest seasons. By seeing the "big picture" of learning opportunities that exist within many rural cultures, teachers will not view these activities as interruptions to learning but, rather, integrate these events into the curriculum as occasions to learn and practice research or employment and marketing skills, to advance writing skills, or to apply mathematical concepts. Rural parents also place a high value on sports activities and other competitions common to rural areas such as those associated with 4-H programs. Teachers who are able to integrate these activities and interests into the school curricula are able to connect academic learning to rural life and culture. Rural communities like to see teachers involved in school and community events.

Those who teach in rural areas served by migrant workers should be aware that migrant students attend a particular school for only a few weeks at a time before relocating. This transience presents a real challenge to rural teachers who must make special efforts to foster a welcoming classroom environment to integrate migrant and local students into a cohesive community of learners. The rural teacher will face additional instructional challenges with migrant children who often speak little or no English. Fostering conti-

Working with family members and students who live in rural communities can present teachers and school administrators with unique challenges and opportunities. What are some of these challenges and opportunities?

nuity in students' learning programs is yet another challenge. Teachers of migrant children could easily provide "take-along learning activities" to migrant students when they move on to the next school as a way to encourage students to practice learned skills. Parents could be encouraged to present these reinforcement activities to the child's next teacher to provide instructional continuity.

Teachers in rural communities will find themselves in cultures that are as distinctly different as those in international locations. The school is an integral part of the community and teachers are often looked upon as leaders and role models. Rural teachers need to be able to communicate with parents and other members of the community without using intimidating vocabulary. Teachers need to act professionally without distancing themselves by behavior that may be interpreted as "putting on airs." Some parents and family members in rural areas may not be literate. Some homes will not have phone service. Because of distance and farm chores, many parents will be unable to attend meetings at school. Although time consuming, making home visits may be the only way a teacher will be able to communicate with a child's caregiver. Strong home–school ties based on mutual respect and cooperation will result in a quality education for all children regardless of their racial, ethnic, or cultural backgrounds.

All students from racial and ethnic minorities come to school with rich cultural backgrounds and learning competencies steeped in the traditions of family and community. These culturally embedded learning competencies are the most significant skills minority children bring to school. Culturally responsive educators, however, struggle with providing a balance between accepting and respecting the unique characteristics of minority students and preparing them for postschool environments in the mainstream American culture. In fact, some people believe that culturally and linguistically diverse students need to embrace mainstream American culture and be taught according to mainstream learning expectations to increase their chances of assuming promising careers where they will be expected to display values and norms of mainstream American culture (Eisenhart & Cutts-Dougherty, 1991; Franklin, 1992; Gollnick & Chinn, 1990).

Culturally responsive teachers can begin to balance respect for students' cultures and prepare them for living in real-world settings by adapting their instructional programs to accommodate students' cultural learning styles and needs. Teachers can increase learning opportunities for all of their students by ensuring that their instruction is context embedded, content rich, equitable, interactive, and experiential (Correa, Blanes-Reyes, & Rapport, 1995).

Lessons that are context embedded contain information that is compatible with the sociocultural backgrounds of students. For example, migrant children who have never visited large city centers might have difficulty relating to social studies textbooks and readers that focus on families who live in high-rise apartment buildings and ride metro rails to school and work. Children attending inner-city schools who have never traveled far from their neighborhoods might have difficulty relating to stories about migrant families whose lives revolve around farms and orchards. Teachers can help students relate to unfamiliar materials and environments by using interactive and experiential teaching strategies. As the earlier discussion about different cultural groups indicated, most students learn more effectively by participating in hands-on experiential activities as members of a learning team. This instructional approach allows the teacher to provide needed assistance as students assume responsibility for their own learning.

Teachers also can help students learn more easily by providing content-rich curriculum that shows students how to apply learning to their daily lives. Education that is relevant to students encourages them to develop a positive attitude, and builds pride in their cultural heritage. Culturally responsive schools and teachers believe that all children can and should learn regardless of their cultural backgrounds.

CONCLUSION

Although teachers of children from culturally different backgrounds face many challenges in providing them with a quality education, these challenges are not insurmountable. Culturally sensitive practices that include teaching, learning, and performance strategies compatible with the sociocultural backgrounds of students will ensure their access to information and learning. In

The culturally responsive classroom is structured to accommodate the learning needs of students from various cultural backgrounds. Culturally responsive classrooms integrate the traditions and cultural norms of students during instruction throughout the school year.

general, students from minorities prefer to learn through hands-on activities and cooperative learning groups. These arrangements change patterns of classroom instruction from teacher monologues to instructional conversations that permit freer, more open dialogue between peers and among all students and the teacher.

APPLICATION
Working with Families

Teachers who take the time to become aware of students' cultural heritages and incorporate them into instruction will be rewarded with family members who are willing to communicate and interact with school personnel. Strong parental support can be nurtured in a school atmosphere in which family involvement is valued and parents feel like they are part of a team. Parent centers, for example, should be located close to the principal's office near the entrance of the school rather than in a trailer away from the main building. Welcome banners, bright colors, and a neat, orderly atmosphere in the parent center will encourage parents to return.

Invite parents and family members to bring in examples of their culture's food, dress, or traditions to share with the class. Prepare a classroom map with colored pins to indicate students' countries of origin. Migrant students may want to prepare and discuss for the class a map showing their travels through the various agricultural regions of the country.

Plan a community celebration with teachers, staff, and parents at the school focusing on a cultural event such as Chinese New Year, Cinco de Mayo, or a fall harvest. Families should be encouraged to play a major role in the planning and carrying out of these activities.

Encourage activities that families can do with their children to foster the connection between home and school. Send home calendars or newsletters that describe fun activities reflecting the curricular topics for the month that families can do together. To encourage literacy development, ask children to make up shopping lists with their parents, or read the newspaper together looking for advertisements of grocery sale items. Suggest that migrant families keep a notebook of their travels to which students can add their impressions. Encourage students to collect family histories and folktales from their culture. There are a number of excellent books dealing with different cultures that students can check out of the library to read with their families. (See Appendix A)

Send invitations to families to visit the classroom to observe what their children are learning. For migrant, rural, or homeless families who may not have telephones or transportation, more creative approaches will have to be taken to ensure that they feel welcome. The school may want to arrange a bus to pick up parents or schedule car pools to bring in parents for special visits. Invitations may have to be extended many times to encourage parents who are hesitant to visit the school because they are unsure of the protocol or have negative feelings because of their own past experiences. Another consideration is child care. Perhaps community service groups could volunteer to provide care for younger siblings while their parents participate in planning meetings or teacher–parent conferences.

In some cases, the only way to connect with families may be home visits. Make an appointment with the family to be visited, giving at least a week's notice. The only convenient time for a visit may be a Saturday morning or Sunday afternoon. Take along some examples of the student's work that are exemplary to provide a positive tone to the conversation. Share information about the student's talents and strengths. Ask for information about the student's interests and talents. Let the parent do more of the talking and listen carefully for clues about how best to connect with the family. Students will be pleased to see that their parents are valued by the school.

The case study that follows concerns a student from a different culture who faces problems fitting in with some of her mainstream classmates. All students find it difficult when their families relocate, requiring them to change schools and adjust to a new group of friends. These demands are even more challenging for students from minoritity cultures who, in addition to dealing with typical demands, must cope with being culturally different. Schools can have a significant impact on how easily and well minority students are integrated into the school community. The names of the characters have been changed, but the situation is based on an actual event. As a teacher, you are likely to encounter similar situations.

CASE STUDY: *Who Suffers When Cultures Collide?*

Mei-Lin, a new student at Wilkinson Middle School, had recently moved with her family to central Ohio from Los Angeles. She has lived in the United States for 4 years and speaks English well, but with a notable accent marked by intonation and stress features that differ from standard English.

Mei-Lin enjoyed her team-learning mates; they all accepted her, it seemed, except for Sam who constantly made snide remarks to Mei-Lin and frequently glared at her with squinted eyes and a cocky grin. The other three members of the group were pleasant toward her, especially Margie, her student mentor, who was exceptionally nice. It was Margie who had asked Mr. North to assign Mei-Lin to the "Raiders," the team-learning group to which Margie belonged.

It had been nearly a week since the disturbance occurred in Mr. North's social studies classroom. The students were sitting at their team stations eagerly waiting for Mr. North to announce the winner of the Bluejay Research Project. The teams had worked on their projects during the 3 previous weeks, and earlier that day each of the teams had given their individual reports to the class. The students knew that the team receiving the highest score would be invited to present their project at the PTA meeting next month. As Mr. North announced that the Falcons were the project winners. Sam banged his fist on his desk, stood up, pointed at Mei-Lin, and blurted, "It's all your fault; why'd you have to join our team, anyway?" Startled, Mei-Lin began to cry, jumped from her seat, and ran into the hallway. Margie ran after her. Mr. North followed the girls into the hallway and, in an effort to calm Mei-Lin, explained that Sam was prone to lose his temper easily, and that she should not interpret his behavior as a sign that the other children didn't like her. Even though Mei-Lin continued to cry over the incident, Mr. North ushered the girls back to the classroom where, shortly after, the bell rang dismissing students for the Thanksgiving holiday.

Later that evening Mr. North phoned Mei-Lin's parents to inform them of the incident and to inquire about Mei-Lin. Mr. and Mrs. Nguyen appreciated Mr. North's call. They told him, in broken English, that Mei-Lin had been upset the previous night, saying she was worried about giving her report to the class. They added that she didn't want to go to school that morning but that they insisted she go and do what the teacher wanted her to do. At Mr. North's suggestion, Mr. and Mrs. Nguyen agreed to meet with him after the Thanksgiving holiday to discuss Mei-Lin's situation.

Mr. and Mrs. Nguyen sat quietly in Mr. North's classroom as he explained that the disturbance in Mei-Lin's study group had erupted because of Sam's insensitive behavior toward Mei-Lin, whom he blamed for causing their study team to miss receiving the first-place award. Mr. North apologized for Sam's crude outburst which, he said, was inexcusable. When her parents asked why Mei-Lin had received a low grade for her part of the team project, Mr. North explained that he had to be fair in his grading practice, that each team member contributed a possible 10 points to their team's score for their oral presentation as part of the team assignment, and that because Mei-Lin had failed to give her oral report to the class, 10 points had been deducted from the team's score. Mr. North went on to explain that he had to be rigorous in his grading of this requirement because the state standard for middle school specified that students were to demonstrate competence in oral expression, using standard American English, proper voice control, body language, and so on. Mr. and Mrs. Nguyen thanked Mr. North for taking the time to meet with them. They promised to encourage Mei-Lin to return to school and do what Mr. North expected.

CASE STUDY DISCUSSION GUIDE

Themes: Integrating minority students into the mainstream school culture; sensitizing majority students to the needs of minority students; communicating and collaborating with minority parents.

Actors

A. How would you characterize each of the actors in this case? (List each person's name and give one-, two-, or three-word descriptions for each actor.)

Issues

B. What are the major issues in this case? (Make a list of these issues.)

Probes

1. What could Mr. North have done to create a more culturally responsive classroom environment?
2. What caused the Raiders not to win the first-place award?
3. Was Sam justified in blaming Mei-Lin for causing the Raiders not to win first place?
4. Is Mr. North's grading practice appropriate?
5. Was Mr. North's way of handling the incident appropriate?

C. Why did Mei-Lin leave the classroom?

Probes

1. Was Mei-Lin being too sensitive? Did she overreact to Sam's remark?
2. Was Sam's behavior typical of a middle school student?
3. Are teachers responsible for the behavior of their students?

D. Was Mr. North's response to Mei-Lin's parents appropriate?

Probes

1. Did Mr. North "go the extra mile" by phoning Mei-Lin's parents to check on her condition and arranging to meet with them after the holidays to discuss her unhappiness at school?
2. What is the evidence that Mr. North is a culturally sensitive teacher?
3. Mr. North said he had to "be fair" in his grading practice. What does that mean?
4. Was Mr. North being fair to Mei-Lin when he gave her a zero for not giving the oral report? Was this an act of fairness to Mei-Lin's classmates?
5. Is there more than one way to require students to demonstrate competence? If so, would it be fair to allow such a practice?
6. There is the issue of Mr. North's responsibility for preparing his students to meet state requirements in oral expression. Is Mr. North acting responsibly by giving Mei-Lin an opportunity to develop this competence?

Problems or Conflicts

What are the problems or conflicts in this case? Make a list of these problems or conflicts and specify whether you think they stem from personal or institutional origins. Now, examine the list further. Can you separate the items on your list into primary and secondary subcategories? (After completing this last step, you may find it easier to suggest solutions to the problems or conflicts in this case.)

Solutions

How could the problems in this case have been avoided? If you had been one of the actors in this case, what would you have done differently?

Probes

1. What factors need to be considered by teachers when they group students for cooperative learning activities?
2. Knowing that Sam could be rude and easily lose his temper, should Mr. North have assigned Mei-Lin and Sam to the same learning team? Was the group's task appropriate?
3. Could Mr. North have helped Mei-Lin prepare to meet the state standard for demonstrating competence in oral expression without insisting that she give a report in a competitive context?
4. Prior to the incident, how could Mr. and Mrs. Nguyen have become involved in helping Mei-Lin adjust to her new school?

SUPPLEMENTAL ACTIVITIES

FIELD EXPERIENCE A

School-Based Activity

As you observe and participate in schools, look for behaviors, events, and activities that reflect cultural pluralism. You may want to focus your inquiries and observations on one or more of the following.

1. Interview the principal or guidance counselor and find out (a) the different minority groups that are part of the school population; (b) whether there are written guidelines for integrating students from minority's families into the school community, and if so, what those guidelines are; (c) what concessions are made for students and parents who do not communicate well in English; and (d) what staff development is provided to educate teachers about the needs of minority students and families, and strategies for accommodating those needs.

2. Interview three different teachers in their classrooms and ask how they accommodate the cultural learning styles of their students from minorities. Observe the classroom environment for signs of cultural sensitivity. Ask how cultural differences are integrated into the instructional program. Are these activities

integrated throughout the school year or are they limited to specific parts of the curriculum? Ask how minority parents and other family members are involved in the instructional program. What religious and national holidays of minority students are recognized or celebrated at school?

FIELD EXPERIENCE B

Community-Based Activity

Look for community cultural events you can attend. These might include religious holidays, New Year's celebrations, parades, food fairs, or dance presentations. Reflect on your feelings as a stranger at the event. Do you know what behavior is expected? Can you understand the language(s) being spoken? Are you comfortable asking someone for information about the event or occasion?

RESPONSE JOURNAL
PROMPTS

As an alternative to using the **Case Study Discussion Guide,** reflect on the case and construct a written response to the following prompts:

1. Think of five things Mr. North could have done to protect Mei-Lin from the embarrassment she suffered and integrate these suggestions into a creative position response.

2. Do you think Mr. North communicated properly with Mr. and Mrs. Nguyen? Take a position: Justify his behavior, or offer recommendations for how the communication could have been improved.

3. What role do Mr. and Mrs. Nguyen have in seeing that Mei-Lin has a smooth transition into her new school? What kind of collaboration should they expect from Mei-Lin's teacher and school officials?

ROLE PLAYING AND
REFLECTION EXERCISE

To better understand cultural differences in the classroom, participate in a role playing scenario depicting a dialogue between two teachers, one groping for ways to create a culturally sensitive classroom environment and the other assuming a laissez-faire position. One teacher could argue some of the research-based reasons for integrating culturally sensitive practices into classroom events, whereas the other could disagree, citing two or three obstacles to accommodating the cultural learning needs of all students in the typical classroom. Following the role playing, break into small groups to discuss the conflicting positions and empathize with the positions of both teachers; expand both of their lists.

DISCUSSION
Identify practical ways to (a) implement culturally sensitive practices, and (b) remove or mitigate obstacles to creating culturally sensitive practices.

IMPLICATIONS FOR FAMILY INVOLVEMENT

Following the brainstorming activity, construct a list of ways a teacher's efforts to create a culturally sensitive classroom environment may influence the nature of family involvement and, in fact, how one might affect the other. You may want to modify your lists after listening to the comments and insights of your peers.

REFERENCES

Au, K., & Kawakami, A. (1985). Research currents: Talk story and learning to read. *Language Arts, 62,* 406–411.

Au, K., & Mason, J. (1983). Cultural congruence in classroom participation: Achieving a balance of rights. *Discourse Process, 6,* 145–167.

Bellah, R. N., Madsen, R., Sullivan, W. M., Swidler, A., & Tipton, S. M. (1985). *Habits of the heart: Individualism and commitment in American life.* New York: Harper & Row.

Charlesworth, R. (1996). *Understanding child development* (2nd ed.). Albany, NY: Delmar.

Chase, R. (2001). *Connecting public schools with communities in post-September 11 America: Parental and family involvement in education.* Address given to the National Press Club, November 16, 2001, Washington, DC.

Council on American-Islamic Relations. (1997). *An educator's guide to Islamic religious practices.* Washington, DC.

D'Andrea, M. D., & Daniels, J. (1997). Continuing the discussion about racism. *Aces Spectrum, 58,* 8–9.

Diss, R. E. (2001). *Preparing teachers for rural schools: What's different?* Paper presented at the National Conference of the American Association of Colleges for Teacher Education, Dallas, TX.

Dunn, R., & Griggs, S. (1996). Hispanic-American students and learning style. (Eric Document Reproduction Service No. ED 393607)

Dunn, L., & Kontos, S. (1997). What have we learned about developmentally appropriate practice? *Young Children, 52* (5), 4–13. Journal of the National Association for the Education of Young Children.

Eisenhart, M. A., & Cutts-Dougherty, K. (1991). Social and cultural constraints on students' access to school knowledge. In E. H. Hiebert (Ed.), *Literacy for a diverse society: Perspectives, practices, and policies.* New York: Teachers College Press.

Elkind, D. (1988, January). Educating the very young: A call for clear thinking. *NEA Today,* 22–27.

Foster, H. (1986). *Ribbin', jivin' and playin' the dozens.* New York: Ballantine Books.

Franklin, M. E. (1992). Culturally sensitive practices for African-American learners with disabilities. *Exceptional Children, 59,* 115–122.

Gay, G. (1995). African-American culture and contributions in American life. In C. A. Grant (Ed.), *Educating for diversity: An anthology of multicultural voices* (35–52). Boston: Allyn & Bacon.

Gilbert, S. E., & Gay, G. (1983). Improving the success in school of poor black children. In B. J. R. Shade (Ed.), *Culture, style and the educative process* (pp. 275–283). Springfield, IL: Charles C. Thomas.

Gollnick, D. M., & Chinn, P. C. (1990). *Multicultural education in a pluralistic society* (3rd ed.). Upper Saddle River, NJ: Merrill/Prentice Hall.

Hanna, J. (1988). *Disruptive school behavior: Class, race and culture.* New York: Holmes & Meier.

Henry, W. (1990, April 9). Beyond the melting pot. *Time,* 28.

Irvine, J. J. & York, D. E. (1995). Learning styles and culturally diverse students: A literature review. In

J. A. Banks (Ed.), *Handbook of research on multicultural education* (pp. 484–497). New York: Simon & Schuster Macmillan.

Jackson, M. L. (1995). Counseling youth of Arab ancestry. In C. C. Lee (Ed.), *Counseling for diversity* (pp. 41–60). Needham Heights, MA: Allyn & Bacon.

Kim, M., Shin, H., & Cai, D. (1998). Cultural influence: The preferred forms of requesting and rerequesting. *Communications Monographs, 65,* 47–82.

Ladson-Billings, G. (1999). Preparing teachers for diverse populations: A critical race theory perspective. In A. Iran-Nejad & P. D. Pearson (Eds.), *Review of research in education,* 24. Washington, DC: American Educational Research Association.

Leung, E. K. (1988). Cultural and acultural commonalities and diversities among Asian Americans: Identification and programming considerations. In A. A. Ortiz & B. A. Ramirez (Eds.), *Schools and the culturally diverse exceptional student: Promising practices and future directions* (pp. 86–95). Reston, VA: Council for Exceptional Children.

Lewis, A. (2003, May). Accountability on the backs of rural children. *Phi Delta Kappan, 84*(9), 643–644.

Mackelprang, R., & Salsgiver, R. (1999). *Disability: A diversity model approach in human service practice.* Pacific Grove, CA: Brooks/Cole.

Martel, L. D. (1998). *Theories of learning styles, neurosciences, guided imagery, suggestopaedia, multiple intelligences, and integrative learning.* Paper presented to the New York State Board of Regents' Panel on Learning Styles. New Haven, CT: Yale University Institute for Social and Policy Studies.

Mason, T. C. (1999). Prospective teachers' attitudes toward urban schools: Can they be changed? *Multicultural Education, 6*(4), 9–13.

Meece, J. L. (2002). *Child & adolescent development for educators* (2nd ed.). Boston: McGraw-Hill.

Moore, J. A. (1996). *Empowering student teachers to teach from a multicultural perspective.* Paper presented at the Annual Meeting of the American Association of Colleges for Teacher Education, Chicago. (ERIC Document Reproduction Service No. ED 394979)

National Council on Disability (1996, April 26). Improving the implementation of the Individuals with Disabilities Act: Making schools work for all of America's Children. Washington, D.C.: Author.

National Education Association. (1998, September). *Status of public education in rural areas and small towns: A comparative analysis.* Available from http://www.nea.org/publiced/rural.html

Ogbu, J. U. (1988). Cultural diversity and human development. In D. T. Slaughter (Ed.), *Black children and poverty* (pp. 11–28). San Francisco: Jossey-Bass.

Ramirez, M., & Castaneda, A. (1974). *Cultural democracy, bicognitive development and education.* New York: Academic Press.

Roopnarine, J. L., & Johnson, J. E. (2000). *Approaches to early childhood education.* Upper Saddle River, NJ: Merrill/Prentice Hall.

Sawyer, D. (1991). Native learning styles: Shorthand for instructional adaptations? *Canadian Journal of Native Education, 18*(1), 91–104.

Sluglett, P. (2002). Middle East. *In Microsoft Encarta Online Encyclopedia 2002.* Retrieved March 16, 2002, from http://www.encarta.msn.com

Srebalus, D. J., & Brown, D. (2001). *A guide to the helping professions.* Boston: Allyn & Bacon.

Sue, D. W., & Sue, D. (1990). *Counseling the culturally different: Theory and practice* (2nd ed.). New York: Wiley.

Sugai, G. (1988). Educational assessment of culturally diverse and behavior disordered students: An examination of critical effect. In A. A. Ortiz & B. A. Ramirez (Eds.), *Schools and culturally diverse exceptional students.* Reston, VA: Council for Exceptional Children.

Sugai, G., & Maheady, L. (1988, Fall). Cultural diversity and individual assessment for behavior disorders. *Teaching Exceptional Children,* 27–31.

Suleiman, M. F. (1996). *Educating the Arab American child: Implications for teachers.* Unpublished manuscript, Fort Hays State University, College of Education, Hays, KS.

Tharp, R., & Gallimore, R. (1988). *Rousing minds to life: Teaching, learning and schooling in social context.* New York: Cambridge University Press.

Turnbull, A. P., Turnbull, H. R., Shank, M., & Leal, D. (1995). *Exceptional lives: Special education in today's schools* (p. 8). Upper Saddle River, NJ: Merrill/Prentice Hall.

Yee, L. Y. (1988). Asian children. *Teaching Exceptional Children, 20*(4), 49–50.

Young, L. S., & Edwards, P. A. (1996). Parents, families, and communities: Opportunities for preservice teacher education. In F. B. Murray (Ed.), *The teacher educator's handbook.* San Francisco: Jossey-Bass.

5

UNDERSTANDING NONTRADITIONAL FAMILIES

The school is the mirror of society and of the family. As society and the family change, so too must the school.

—David Elkind, 1995

CHANGING FAMILY STRUCTURES

Teachers face the challenge of educating an increasingly diverse student population from a variety of home environments and family structures. Common contemporary family structures include two-parent nuclear families, single-parent families, blended families, extended or intergenerational families, families headed by gay male or lesbian partners, and foster families. (See Chapter 1, where this topic was initially introduced in a discussion of the contemporary family.) With only 31% of contemporary families fitting the description of a nuclear family consisting of a father, mother, and two children (Outtz, 1993; Tutwiler, 1998), teachers must provide and maintain a variety of family participation opportunities to involve all of their students' families. The following discussion of family structures will help teachers understand their unique features.

TWO-PARENT NUCLEAR FAMILIES

The number of two-parent nuclear families has been steadily decreasing over the past 29 years (Santrock, 2001). White, non-Hispanic children are more likely than African American children and somewhat more likely than Hispanic children to live with two parents. In 2000, 77% of White, non-Hispanic children lived with two parents, compared with 38% of African American children and 65% of children of Hispanic origin (Federal Interagency Forum on Child and Family Statistics, 2001). Older children also are less likely to live with two parents. Sixty-six percent of children ages 15 to 17 lived with one parent in 2000 (Federal Interagency Forum on Child and Family Statistic, 2001).

SINGLE-PARENT FAMILIES

The most common contemporary nonnuclear family structure is the one-parent family headed by either never-married or divorced parents. Twenty-three percent of families in the United States are headed by single parents, a percentage higher than in all other countries (Santrock, 2001). In 1999 nearly 28% of all children in the United States under the age of 18 lived in a one-parent household (U.S. Census Bureau, 1999). Of this number, 83% lived with mothers (40% of whom had never been married), and 17% lived with fathers (33% of whom had never been married; U.S. Census Bureau). What do these statistics mean to the classroom teacher? Single parents have less time to spend attending to family matters because they have full responsibility for serving their family's needs. After a full day of work, maintaining a household, and providing for the basic needs of their children, single parents may lack the energy to participate in school programs. They may also lack the material resources to leave the home and become involved. Seeing that homework assignments are completed may be the most reasonable way single parents can be involved in their children's education, especially if there are two or more children living in the household.

When compared to children in two-parent families, it is not surprising that children in single-parent households have significantly less parent involvement in their school activities across grade levels (U.S Department of Health and Human Services [HHS], 2000). Children from single-parent families have lower grades and attendance records than children from two-parent families, and their school dropout rates are twice as high (McLanahan & Sandefur, 1994).

TEENAGE MOTHERS

Some single parents are teenagers who never married. Even though the number of adolescent pregnancies in the United States has decreased by 3% since 1991 (Curtin & Martin, 2000), 13% of the births during both 1997 and 1998 were by teenagers between the ages of 13 and 19 (HHS, 2000). The actual number of adolescent mothers who are raising children in single-parent homes is not known. However, regardless of whether adolescent mothers live alone with their children or within some other family structure, the needs of adolescent single mothers are even more critical than those of older single mothers. In addition to many of the constraints faced by older single mothers, adolescent mothers must face consequences likely to include dropping out of school, living in poverty, and, if heading their own households, raising a child without the help and guidance of more experienced family members (Furstenberg, Brooks-Gunn, & Chase-Lansdale, 1989.) Additionally, babies of adolescent mothers are frequently born prematurely or of low birth weight as a result of poor nutrition or inadequate prenatal care. These children commonly experience physical problems in early infancy. These children also are known to have a higher incidence of learning and psychological problems during their early school years, and more achievement and discipline problems during adolescence, than do children born of older single mothers (Hack, Klein, & Taylor, 1995).

BLENDED FAMILIES

Households consisting of divorced and remarried parents with children from previous marriages are confronted with a unique set of challenges. Children in blended families commonly face increased difficulties adjusting to new authority figures, stepsiblings, new family rules, the divided attention of parents, and, frequently, new neighborhoods and friends. They bring family history and traditions that must be blended into the new family's expectations (Fuller & Marxen, 1998). When children are unable to cope with the demands of living in a blended family, they may experience academic problems, lower self-esteem, and social problems. These students are also more vulnerable to opportunities to engage in delinquent activity (Anderson, Greene, Hetherington, & Clingempeel, 1999; Hetherington, 2000).

Young adolescents, already preoccupied with autonomy and identity issues, commonly find it especially difficult adjusting to the demands of living in blended families (Hetherington, 1995). To help students deal with the difficulties of adjusting to a new family, teachers may provide opportunities for students to discuss and express their feelings, encourage supportive communication, use curriculum materials that present positive images of blended families, and keep parents informed about their children's progress and difficulties (Frieman, 1993, 1997).

This picture of the two-parent family is becoming less and less common in American society. What challenges do contemporary schools face due to the ever increasing numbers of students being raised in nontraditional families?

Teachers who are aware of the increased demands placed on children living in blended families will be better able to discuss their academic performance and social behavior with parents.

EXTENDED OR INTERGENERATIONAL FAMILIES

An increasingly common family structure is the extended or intergenerational family. The composition of this family type may include members from more than one household or several generations of offspring, with a grandparent most commonly being the primary caregiver. The exceptions to the grandparent being the primary caregiver are Native American households (U.S. Census Bureau, 1993) and Asian American families (Chan, 1992), where one or both birth parents share child-rearing responsibilities with other family members.

An estimated four million children in the United States are being raised by a grandparent or extended family member (U.S. Census Bureau, 1999). Twelve percent of these children are being raised in African American homes by grandmothers, 6% in Hispanic households, and 4% in White, non-Hispanic households. One quarter of the birth parents of children being raised by grandparents in 1999 were completely out of their children's lives (Szinovacz, 1998).

Although some grandparents receive help from other family members to raise their grandchildren, many do not. They must, therefore, seek help from social agencies and other support groups (Kluger & Aprea, 1999). Many grandparents will become highly involved in their grandchildren's school activities, but some will be limited by advanced age and physical restrictions. Additionally, some grandparents may lack the educational background and experience to help their grandchildren with homework. To involve grandparents in the schooling activities of their grandchildren, schools must examine their policies and practices to see how "grandfamily" friendly those policies and practices are (Rothenberg, 1996). These practices might include information about obtaining health and social services, afterschool programs, optional ways to become involved in school, and networking connections to help with the demands of child rearing.

FAMILIES HEADED BY GAY MALE AND LESBIAN PARENTS

Social scientists maintain that the number of children being raised in gay male and lesbian households has steadily increased over the past few decades. Informed estimates of numbers are hard to come by, however, because of the prevailing stigma associated with homosexuality and, therefore, a reluctance among gay male and lesbian parents to identify themselves. When gay male and lesbian parents do disclose their sexual orientation, they tend to do so when living in communities that are open and supportive of diverse lifestyles (Casper, Schultz, & Wickens, 1992). Because of negative attitudes toward homosexuality, gay male and lesbian parents may experience high levels of stress due to their sexual orientation, regardless of whether they conceal or disclose their sexual preference and lifestyle. One significant reason why many gay male and lesbian parents are reluctant to disclose their sexual orientation is fear of losing custody of their children. Yet, children raised in gay male and lesbian households are no different than children raised in heterosexual homes in terms of their social relations with peers and adults, social competence, self-concept, and moral judgments. Similarly, research indicates very few differences between children of gay male and lesbian parents and heterosexual parents, including gender identity, role, or sexual orientation (Patterson & Chan, 1999; Tasker & Golombok, 1997).

Teachers can show sensitivity toward students raised in gay male and lesbian households by maintaining a nonjudgmental attitude toward their parents, safeguarding against their vulnerability to peer teasing, and using the term *parent* rather than *mother* or *father*. They may also ensure that the nature of classroom and homework assignments reflects a variety of family structures.

FOSTER FAMILIES

More than half a million children live with foster families (Noble, 1997). Predominantly children of color and residents of urban areas, nearly all have experienced neglect and abuse. Because foster children are moved frequently, often from one foster family to another, they have to adjust to school changes, different curricula, and new teachers. Additionally, they may be grieving over being separated from their biological families (Ayasse, 1995; Brodkin & Coleman, 1996; Lindsay, Chadwick, Landsverk, & Pierce, 1993). Adults who decide to become foster parents do so for many reasons. Some want to provide good homes for children in need, some want companionship, some may have been foster children themselves, and some erroneously expect to benefit financially (Stahl, 1990). However, many discover that the children assigned to them have needs for which they are inadequately trained to meet. Additionally, they are obligated to follow the strict rules of a social welfare system that often provides little support and inadequate funds. A growing segment of foster parents are grandparents or other relatives of children whose biological parents cannot take care of them (Okun, 1996).

Teachers of foster children can be more effective if they know about the problems children and their foster families are experiencing and how these problems affect their learning. The involvement of foster parents is critical in providing a successful school experience for these children because the parents usually know the most about their children's lives and can work in tandem with the teachers (Noble, 1997; Stahl, 1990). Teachers should encourage foster parents to help children with their homework and see that they attend school regularly.

THE DYNAMICS OF FAMILY INTERACTION

A more complete understanding of the dynamics of family behavior may be obtained by considering the family from a social systems, or ecological, perspective. This perspective views the family as a reciprocal system of interacting members, each of whom affects the other, thereby contributing to its social environment and functioning. This mutual-impact theory postulates that just as family members influence the behaviors of one another, so too is there a reciprocal relationship between families and other social structures within the broader community, each one affecting the other. According to this theory, the environment is a series of social systems that interact with each other in complex ways to form increased complex social environments (Bronfenbrenner, 1986; Bronfenbrenner & Morris, 1998). Understanding the unique ways families interact can provide teachers with subtle, yet important, interactive cues to direct home–school communication and community involvement.

The ways in which family members interact with one another are known to create a social climate that, over time, establishes a family's interactive pattern. As this pattern "takes root," family members learn social expectations and interactive skills (Patterson, DeBaryshe, & Ramsey, 1989). The following scenario illustrates how the reciprocal interactive behavior of family members influences one another's social behavior:

1. A girl teases her older brother, who makes her stop teasing by yelling at her (yelling is negatively reinforced).

2. A few minutes later, the girl calls her brother a nasty name. The boy then chases and hits her.

3. The girl stops calling him names (which negatively reinforces hitting). She then whimpers and hits him back, and he withdraws (negatively reinforcing her hits). The boy then approaches and hits his sister again, and the conflict escalates.

4. At this point, the mother intervenes. However, her children are too emotionally disturbed to listen to reason, so she finds herself applying punitive and coercive tactics to make them stop fighting.

5. The fighting stops (thus reinforcing the mother for using coercive methods). However, the children now begin to whine, cry, or yell at the mother. These counter coercive techniques are then reinforced if the mother backs off and accepts peace at any price. Unfortunately, backing off is only a temporary solution. The next time that the children antagonize each other and become involved in an unbearable conflict, the mother is likely to use even more coercion to get them to stop. The children once again apply their own methods of counter coercion to induce her to "lay off," and the family atmosphere becomes increasingly unpleasant for everyone.[1]

Recent reforms of the nation's welfare program serve as an example of the reciprocal impact that families and agencies within the larger community have

---

[1]From *Developmental Psychology. Childhood and Adolescence* 4th edition by Shaffer. Copyright 1996. Reprinted with permission of Wadsworth, a division of Thomson Learning: www.thomsonrights.com. Fax 800 730–2215.

on one another. As back-to-work requirements were initiated in the mid-1990's to help families on public assistance become more independent, the demand for training and work programs increased. These programs had an impact not only on the family but also on educational and employment services. Many single- and two-parent families experienced tremendous change when family members could no longer stay home to care for their young children. As parents returned to school, participated in training programs, and reentered the workplace, the need for early child-care services increased. Because most of those who participated in the back-to-work program did not earn enough to pay for child-care services, family health needs, and expenses associated with returning to work, the government had to provide additional legislative and financial support. In turn, the results of this intervention had an impact on self-sufficient families and the marketplace as public monies were used to support the program.

As a result of the many systems that influence and change families, children are challenged to cope with and adjust to changing family structures, new schools, friends, and cultural expectations (Bronfenbrenner, 1986). Whereas some children can cope with these challenges easily and well, others cannot. Teachers who understand how reciprocal relationships between social structures can influence families have an opportunity to help students cope with these demands by directing them and their families to available support systems, and by offering involvement opportunities suited to their needs (Pianta, 1999).

PARENTING STYLES

The way family members interact with one another may also explain student social behavior at school. The household social environment in which children are raised teaches and reinforces interactive patterns and social behavior (Miller, Cowan, Cowan, Hetherington, & Clingempeel, 1993; Patterson et al., 1989). Because interactive patterns are aligned with parenting styles, the following review of common parenting behaviors will supply additional information about the uniqueness of families and their systemic-driven social behavior.

Many studies of family socialization have examined the effect of parenting practices on child development. A review of these studies (Maccoby & Martin, 1983) identified two particular dimensions of parenting behavior: whether they were strict (controlling) or permissive (gave a great deal of autonomy), and whether they were accepting and responsive or rejecting and unresponsive. Based upon these two dimensions, four parenting styles were identified. Baumrind (1971) identified three parenting styles—authoritarian, authoritative, and permissive—the latter of which was later divided into two forms, permissive neglectful and permissive indulgent (Maccoby & Martin, 1983).

Authoritarian parenting is characterized by a highly controlling, punitive style in which parents insist that children follow directions and meet their demands. Little verbal exchange is allowed. Authoritarian parents are highly involved in their children's lives for the purpose of restricting their behavior to ensure that parental demands are met. Children are given few choices.

Children develop self-confidence and social competence through positive interactions with family members. In what ways is this single mother contributing to her childrens' social development?

Children raised in authoritarian homes generally lack social competence and self-confidence, and frequently initiate aggressive behavior.

Permissive neglectful parenting is characterized by a lack of involvement in their children's lives. Typically, these parents give children lots of freedom and very little supervision. Their dealings with their children generally lack warmth. They do not spend much time talking to their children, and they fail to display nurturing behavior. Rather, they communicate the message to their children that other parental involvements are more important than they are. Children raised by permissive neglectful parents generally lack social competence, show poor self-control, and fail to handle independence well.

Permissive indulgent parenting is characterized by a high level of involvement in children's lives, but without placing demands or controls on them. Although permissive indulgent parents display warmth and nurturing behavior, they allow their children to do as they please, with the result that their children find it difficult to control their behavior and expect to always get their way. For this reason, children raised by this parenting style tend to be socially incompetent.

Authoritative parenting is characterized by helping children attain independence through goal achievement, to think for themselves, and to initiate socially acceptable activity. These parents place high demands on their children to achieve realistic academic and social goals, and monitor their behavior consistently to help them achieve those goals. They also encourage extensive verbal exchange to help their children reason through different points of view and make rational choices. They are warm, caring, and nurturing toward their children, demonstrating both love and limits. Authoritative parents tend to produce highly competent children.

IMPACT OF PARENTING STYLES ON FAMILY INVOLVEMENT

Each of the above parenting styles provides a context for understanding how social environments are formed and reinforced in families. The features of these parenting styles also provide direction for establishing effective lines of communication between family members and school personnel (Steinberg, Lamborn, Darling, Mounts, & Dornbusch, 1994). The following ideas may be helpful in achieving this goal.

Authoritarian parents will likely be cooperative with teachers' expectations for involvement as long as these expectations support their own wishes and goals for their children. These parents will be especially supportive when asked to encourage their children to obey school rules and to comply with academic demands. Children who are raised in authoritarian households may display noncompliant and aggressive behavior. Teachers need to provide social opportunities for these children that enable them to demonstrate their unique strengths and positive attributes. These children will also need lots of encouragement and direction to make appropriate choices, especially when these choices are likely to have lasting impacts on their social and academic lives. Teachers will also help these students immeasurably by modeling prosocial behavior and by giving them opportunities to do the same. Teachers should also monitor these students for signs of physical and psychological abuse, and provide appropriate assistance when necessary.

When dealing with parents who display permissive (negligent and indulgent) parenting behavior, teachers will want to provide specific and detailed involvement requests accompanied by frequent reminders and monitoring contacts. Anticipating that these parents may readily offer excuses for failing to follow through on involvement promises, teachers will want to initially involve them in short-term tasks. Once they have been successful at these involvement experiences, they may be encouraged to participate in activities requiring greater degrees of commitment.

Children raised in permissive homes will benefit from learning experiences that enable them to maintain focus and complete short-term, attainable tasks. These children will also need support to comply with classroom and school rules, perhaps by employing a system of rewards and sanctions. This will help students establish compliant behavior patterns and acceptance among their peers.

Authoritative parents will expect the school to have high, yet reasonable, academic and social expectations. They will likely be highly involved in school activities, and hold school administrators and teachers accountable for their

Some households establish daily routines for doing school work. How can school personnel get parents to provide the home support students need to complete school assignments?

children's learning and social progress. Teachers may want to tap the interest and expertise of these parents by involving them in leadership roles to help provide the array of family involvement options that are necessary to accommodate the involvement needs of diverse families. Because authoritative parenting behavior generally produces competent children, teachers will enhance the growth and development of all their students when they reinforce these parenting behaviors in the classroom. Teachers who communicate caring and concern help motivate students to cooperate and comply with their directives and expectations. Similarly, by dealing with disagreements by "talking things out," teachers are likely to establish bonds of mutual respect and trust, while also helping students develop critical thinking and decision-making skills. By exercising authoritative parenting skills in the classroom, teachers will not only attract the involvement of authoritative parents but they will also provide students with the necessary blend of love, rules, expectations, and support that help them structure their lives and become self-reliant, competent adults.

CONCLUSION

The complex and uniquely different character of individual families will require a differentiated approach to involving them in effective home–school partnerships. For certain, "one size fits all" involvement programs will not meet the needs of contemporary families. The vast differences across families will require added vigilance of teachers to anticipate a variety of student needs and opportunities to partner with family members to serve those needs. Whereas this charge asks teachers and school administrators to add to an already "full plate," the benefits of their efforts will surely result in an easier and more productive fulfillment of their existing responsibilities.

APPLICATION

Working with Families

Teachers today must be part educator, part social worker, part psychologist, and part anthropologist. An increasingly diverse student population from nontraditional family structures presents even the most experienced teacher with challenges in establishing meaningful home–school partnerships. The authors recommend that teachers in a school work together to share ideas, resources, and solutions for working with nontraditional families. Partnering with nontraditional families will require that teachers go the extra mile to reduce barriers to communication.

Teachers can use literature as a primary strategy for connecting with nontraditional families and helping students feel comfortable about their family structure. There are a number of excellent books on the market that address a broad continuum of different family structures including single parents, blended families, intergenerational families, foster families, and gay male and lesbian parents (see the section in Appendix A for suggestions on literature for children and adolescents). Teachers can encourage students to check out books that depict their family structures to read with family members. Hopefully, reading the stories together will serve as a springboard to discuss their family's unique qualities. Reading about other families who are similar to theirs will help students confirm the value of their family structures. Teachers should also look for curriculum materials that present positive images of nontraditional family structures to help students realize that their situations are not unique or abnormal.

Other strategies for communicating with all families that have proven effective are monthly newsletters containing parenting tips, written homework schedules that students can take home each week, and short notes mailed to families praising students for something they have accomplished in class. In scheduling conferences, it will be helpful to consider alternative times, either before school or on weekends, for parents who are unable to take time off from work. Creative solutions may be necessary to meet with those parents who may not have telephones or transportation. Grandparents who are primary caregivers or foster parents may need information about community resources such as afterschool programs, social services, or health services.

When classroom projects limit the participation of some students because of their family structures, they may distance these students from full participation in learning. The case study that follows illustrates how a teacher introduces an instructional activity that is meant to connect students to their families, but his intention backfires when a student has a family secret. The names of the characters have been changed, but the situation is based on an actual event. As a teacher, you are likely to encounter similar situations.

Tom was flabbergasted! Never in a million years had he expected that such a good idea would become such a disaster. He was even more flabbergasted because he got the idea for the historical research project from his Aunt Cindy, a successful fourth-grade teacher in another town.

The project was a simple one, filled with several current "best practices" in education such as active learning, investigative research, writing across the curriculum, and cooperative learning. Additionally, the project taught organizational, interviewing, and sequencing skills. The part that really thrilled Tom was that the activity also involved his students' parents and grandparents. Tom thought the project would be a great family involvement activity.

The activity required students to interview their parents and grandparents to gather information about specific events and experiences during their lives. The experiences across generations could then be compared to provide students with a rich supply of cultural and personal data. The process of gathering the information would help to strengthen bonds between the generations!

When Tom first introduced the idea to his fourth-grade students, they showed lots of interest; in fact, Tom couldn't remember his students being as excited about any other project. He was thrilled by their enthusiasm. Sure, some students had initially voiced some concerns like what if they didn't live near their grandparents, or what if their grandparents were dead. A few students asked if they could interview their stepdads or stepmoms. But, there was no question in Tom's mind that his students were overwhelmingly enthusiastic about the project and eager to begin.

That had been a week ago. Students were coming to school every day since Tom first introduced the project, with stories and reports of the data they were collecting. For example, Susan had reported her amazement upon finding out from her grandmother that a new invention during her childhood years was the television, and that the electric can opener was invented during her mom's childhood years. Susan received some good-natured teasing from her classmates when she admitted that she thought televisions and electric can openers had been around since electricity had been invented! Bo said he had called his grandmother in Fort Lauderdale and found out that a song that was very popular about the time she married his grandfather was called "Moon River." The students responded to Bo's announcement, again good-naturedly, with "thumbs down" and a hearty and unanimous "Boooo!" There had been many such shared reporting incidents during the week, all of which Tom thought were good. He felt pleased that the project was providing a common interest that was having a unifying effect on his students. Then, on Thursday, things changed abruptly.

As Tom started class on Thursday morning, students were, once again, eager to share bits and pieces of their interview findings. Everyone cheered when Justin reported that when his grandfather was in fourth grade, school closed down during the "hay season" so that kids could help bale. The class was equally responsive when Michelle related that her dad frequently skipped school to go fishing. Then, during a brief lull in the chatter, Jack yelled to Kenny, "Hey Kenny, what'd you find out about your past?" The room fell silent as all eyes turned toward Kenny. Kenny sat motionless with a blank look on his face. Then he began to cry. Tears flowed down his cheeks and fell to his desktop. He was obviously bothered by the question and the stares of his classmates.

Tom felt rotten. The reality of the incident hit him like a ton of bricks. He could have kicked himself for his own negligence and lack of sensitivity. He should have anticipated that the research project could have had a devastating impact on Kenny, who had come to the school just 2 months earlier and who was having a difficult time fitting in with his classmates. On top of his social problems, Kenny had other challenges to deal with stemming from his family background. Tom knew about Kenny's family history because the principal had shared this confidential information with him when Kenny was placed in his classroom. He should have known better; he could have spared Kenny from this embarrassment, if only he had thought about Kenny's situation.

CASE STUDY DISCUSSION GUIDE

Themes: Teacher insensitivity toward family diversity; understanding students; teaching tolerance and social skills; selecting appropriate classroom activities; creating psychologically supportive environments.

Actors

A. How would you characterize each of the actors in this case? (List each person's name and give one-, two-, or three-word descriptions for each actor.)

Probes

1. How do you think each of the actors in this case feels?
2. How does Tom feel about his students and teaching?
3. How does Kenny feel about being in Tom's classroom?
4. What does Jack's behavior possibly suggest about himself, or the behaviors of other actors?

Issues

B. What are the major issues in this case? (Make a list of these issues.)

Probes

1. Is Tom a good teacher? Why or why not?
2. Did Kenny overreact to the situation? Won't he have to cope with similar situations in the future?
3. Was Jack's behavior typical for his age? Could Jack's behavior have been anticipated?
4. Do classroom activities always have to be appropriate for all students?

C. What other issues emerge in this case?

Problems or Conflicts

What are the problems or conflicts in this case? Make a list of these problems or conflicts and specify whether you think they stem from personal or institutional origins. Now, examine the list further. Can you separate the items on your list into primary and secondary subcategories? (After completing this last step, you may find it easier to suggest solutions to the problems or conflicts in this case.)

Solutions

How could the problems in this case have been avoided? If you had been one of the actors in this case, what would you have done differently?

Probes

1. What could Tom have done to integrate Kenny into the generational activity?
2. Was Jack's behavior predictable? Could it have been averted?
3. Was Kenny's behavior predictable? Could it have been averted?

SUPPLEMENTAL ACTIVITIES

FIELD EXPERIENCE A   *School-Based Activity*

As you observe and participate in schools, look for behaviors, events, and activities that accommodate the involvement needs of different family structures. You may want to focus your inquiries and observations on one or more of the following questions.

1. Survey schools in your area as to the nature of their parent-involvement programs. Do these programs accommodate various family structures? If not, what are these programs lacking?

2. Does the school provide an orientation program for new families to the school?

3. Do parents have access to teachers and administrators beyond the school day?

4. Are family members invited to make appointments with teachers to visit classrooms?

5. Does the school have a communication system in place that includes methods of communication for illiterate or limited-English-speaking families and families with no phones?

6. Does the school have an adequate communication system for informing all parents about school and classroom rules, school and classroom policy, parent–teacher conferences, and bus and lunch schedules?

7. Is there a resource center that provides parenting information for families and teachers?

8. Is there a procedure for addressing family concerns about student placement and making adjustments when necessary?

9. What procedure is in place for parents to offer suggestions, or ask questions about the school program?

Community-Based Activity

Ask the school counselor or principal for suggestions about local family therapists who might be invited to visit your class to discuss the challenges children face belonging to particular family structures. You may want to collaborate with the school where you are observing to gather a small group of teachers, members of your class, and a panel of family members representing a variety of family structures to discuss their needs and how they can best become involved in school activities. This type of activity would benefit and inform the teachers as well as you and your classmates. Either as part of this activity, or at another time, invite several teachers to meet with your class to discuss how they encourage members of various family structures to participate actively in their children's education.

As an alternative to using the **Case Study Discussion Guide,** you may want to reflect on the case and construct a written response to the following prompts:

1. Describe how you would have introduced the generational research activity to Tom's class.

2. Think of a close friend whose family structure is different from yours. Can you identify differences between how you and your friend are challenged in school? How do each of you cope with the challenges you face?

Participate in a role playing activity with classmates assuming the characters depicted in "How do family structures affect classroom instruction?" As the roles are acted out, note the challenges students face because of the family structure(s) in which they live.

Think about your own family. Can you identify a variety of family types in your immediate or extended family? Ask your parents, or someone from their generation, how many of these same family types were present a generation or two ago (Fuller & Olsen, 1998).

DISCUSSION

Construct a list of the differences between a traditional family and a nontraditional family. Compare your lists with those of two classmates. Discuss the similarities and differences between your lists.

IMPLICATIONS FOR FAMILY INVOLVEMENT
Following the discussion activity, construct a list of implications for family involvement applicable to both family structures.

REFERENCES

Anderson, E., Greene, S. M., Hetherington, E. M., & Clingempeel, W. G. (1999). The dynamics of parental remarriage. In E. M. Hetherington (Ed.), *Coping with divorce, single parenting, and remarriage.* Mahwah, NJ: Erlbaum.

Ayasse, R. H. (1995, October). Addressing the needs of foster children: The Foster Youth Services Program. *Social Work in Education, 117*(4), 207–216.

Baumrind, D. (1971). Current patterns of parental authority. *Developmental Psychology Monograph, 4*(1, P. 2).

Brodkin, A. M., & Coleman, M. (1996, January–February). Kids in crisis: Helping a foster child heal. *Instructor, 105*(5), 34–35.

Bronfenbrenner, U. (1986). Ecology of the family as a context for human development: Research perspectives. *Developmental Psychology, 22*(6), 723–742.

Bronfenbrenner, U., & Morris, P. A. (1998). The ecology of developmental processes. In R. M. Lerner (Ed.), *Handbook of child psychology: Theoretical models of human development* (5th ed., Vol. 1, pp. 993–1028). New York: Wiley.

Casper, V., Schultz, S., & Wickens, E. (1992). Breaking the silence: Lesbian and gay parents and the schools. *Teachers College Record, 94,* 109–137.

Chan, S. (1992). Families with Asian roots. In E. W. Lynch & M. J. Hanson (Eds.), *Developing cross-cultural competence* (pp. 121–150). Baltimore: Brooks.

Curtin, S., & Martin, J. (2000). Births: Preliminary data for 1999. *National Vital Statistics Report, 48*(14). Washington, DC: U.S. Department of Health and Human Services, Centers for Disease Control and Prevention.

Elkind, D. (1995, September). School and family in the postmodern world. *Phi Delta Kappan,* 18.

Federal Interagency Forum on Child and Family Statistics. (2001). *America's children: Key national indicators of well-being.* Washington, DC: U.S. Government Printing Office.

Frieman, B. B. (1993). Separation and divorce: Children want their teachers to know. *Young Children, 48*(6), 58–63.

Frieman, B. B. (1997). Two parents—Two homes. *Educational Leadership, 54*(7), 23–25.

Fuller, M. L., & Marxen, C. (1998). Families and their functions—Past and present. In M. L. Fuller & G. Olsen (Eds.), *Home-school relations: Working successfully with parents and families.* Boston: Allyn & Bacon.

Fuller, M. L., & Olsen, G. (Eds.). (1998). *Home-school relations: Working sucessfully with parents and families.* Boston: Allyn & Bacon.

Furstenberg, F. F., Jr., Brooks-Gunn, J., & Chase-Lansdale, L. (1989). Teenaged pregnancy and childbearing. *American Psychologist, 44,* 313–320.

Hack, M., Klein, N., & Taylor, G. (1995). Long-term developmental outcomes of low birth weight infants. *The Future of Children, 5,* 176–196.

Hetherington, E. M. (1995, March). *The changing American family and the well-being of children.* Paper presented at the meeting of the Society for Research in Child Development, Indianapolis.

Hetherington, E. M. (2000). Divorce. In A. Kazdin (Ed.), *Encyclopedia of psychology.* Washington, DC & New York: American Psychological Association and Oxford University Press.

Kluger, M. P., & Aprea, D. M. (1999). Grandparents raising grandchildren: A description of the families and a special pilot program. *Journal of Gerontological Social Work, 32,* 5–17.

Lindsay, S., Chadwick, J., Landsverk, J., & Pierce, E. (1993, November–December). Computerized health and education passport for children in out-of-home care: The San Diego model. *Child Welfare, 72*(6), 581–594.

Maccoby, E. E., & Martin, J. A. (1983). Socialization in the context of family: Parent-child interaction. In P. H. Mussen (Ed.), *Handbook of child psychology. Vol. 4. Socialization, personality, and social development.* New York: Wiley.

McLanahan, S., & Sandefur, G. (1994). *Growing up with a single parent: What hurts, what helps?* Cambridge, MA: Harvard University Press.

Miller, N. B., Cowan, P. A., Cowan, C. P., Hetherington, E. M., & Clingempeel, W. G. (1993). Externalizing in preschoolers and early adolescents: A cross-study replication of a family model. *Developmental Psychology, 29,* 3–18.

Noble, L. S. (1997, April). The face of foster care. *Educational Leadership, 54*(7), 26–28.

Okun, B. F. (1996). Understanding diverse families: What practitioners need to know. New York: Guilford Press.

Outtz, J. H. (1993). *The demographics of American families.* Santa Monica, CA: Milken Institute for Job and Capital Formation. (ERIC Document Reproduction Service No. ED367726)

Patterson, C. J., & Chan, R. W. (1999). Families headed by lesbian and gay parents. In M. E. Lamb (Ed.), *Nontraditional families.* Hillsdale, NJ: Erlbaum.

Patterson, G. R., DeBaryshe, B. D., & Ramsey, E. (1989). A developmental perspective on antisocial behavior. *American Psychologist, 44,* 329–355.

Pianta, R. (1999). *Enhancing relationships between children and teachers.* Washington, DC: American Psychological Association.

Rothenberg, D. (1996). *Grandparents as parents: A primer for schools* (Report No. EDO-PS-96-8). Urbana, IL: ERIC Clearinghouse on Elementary and Early Childhood Education. (ERIC Document Reproduction Service No. ED401044)

Santrock, J. W. (2001). *Child development* (9th ed.). New York: McGraw-Hill.

Shaffer, D. R. (1996). *Developmental psychology: Childhood and adolescence* (4th ed.). Pacific Grove, CA: Brooks/Cole.

Stahl, P. M. (1990). *Children on consignment: A handbook for parenting foster children and their special needs.* Lexington, MA: Lexington Books.

Steinberg, L. Lamborn, S. D., Darling, N., Mounts, N. S., & Dornbusch, S. M. (1994). Over-time changes in adjustment and competence among adolescents from authoritative, authoritarian, indulgent, and neglectful families. *Child Development, 65,* 754–770.

Szinovacz, M. (1998). Grandparents today: A demographic profile. *The Gerontologist, 38,* 37–52.

Tasker, F. L., & Golombok, S. (1997). *Growing up in a lesbian family: Effects on child development.* New York: Guilford Press.

Tutwiler, S. W. (1998). Diversity among families. In M. L. Fuller & G. Olsen (Eds.), *Home-school relations: Working successfully with parents and families* (pp. 40–66). Boston: Allyn & Bacon.

U.S. Census Bureau. (1993). *We the first Americans* (Series WE-5). Washington, DC: U.S. Government Printing Office.

U.S. Census Bureau. (1999). *Statistical abstract of the United States* (119th ed.). Washington, DC: U.S. Government Printing Office.

U.S. Department of Health and Human Services. (2000). *Trends in the well-being of America's children and youth 1999.* Washington, DC: Author.

U.S. Department of Health and Human Services. (2000). *Trends in the well-being of America's children and youth 2000.* Washington, DC: Author.

6

UNDERSTANDING FAMILIES OF CHILDREN WITH SPECIAL NEEDS

How unpleasing to the eye if all the flowers and plants, the leaves and blossoms, the fruits, the branches and the trees of the garden were all of the same shape and colour!

—From *Selections from the Writings of 'Abdu'l-Bahá,* 1997

FAMILIES WHO HAVE CHILDREN WITH SPECIAL NEEDS

All parents think their children are special, and indeed, they are. But, even though all children are special, not all children have special learning needs. Children who do have special learning needs have abilities that differ from the norm to such an extent that they require a special education to develop those abilities. In this chapter we address students who have special learning needs because they either have a disability, or because they are gifted or talented. As we will see, the families with children who fall into these two categories are usually highly involved in their child's schooling. In fact, they may be quite demanding in their efforts to advocate on behalf of their child's educational interests.

STUDENTS WHO HAVE A DISABILITY

Nationally, about 11% of children in the United States aged birth to 21 qualify as having a disability requiring special education (U.S. Department of Education, 1999). Table 6–1 shows the disability categories according to federal special education laws, the number of students identified as needing special services, and the percentage of students receiving services in each category during the 1997–1998 school year.

The number of children categorized with a specific learning disability increased 40% in the 10-year period from 1989 to 1999, particularly because of the high numbers of children who qualified for special services due to attention-deficit disorders, whereas numbers in the other categories remained relatively consistent (U.S. Department of Education, 2000).

Children who have a disability have been protected by federal laws since 1975 (Education for All Handicapped Children Act, 1975) to ensure that they receive the special education they need. The Individuals with Disabilities Education Act in 1990, and its amendments of 1997 (Individuals with Disabilities Education Act [IDEA], 1990, 1997), represent the government's sustained

Table 6–1

Students requiring special education, 1997–1998.

Type of Disability	Number of Students Identified	Percentage of Students Receiving Service
Specific learning disability	2,726,000	46.2
Speech or language impairment	1,059,000	17.9
Mental retardation	589,000	10.0
Serious emotional disturbance	453,000	7.7
Hearing impairment	69,000	1.2
Orthopedic impairment	67,000	1.1
Other health impairment	190,000	3.2
Visual impairment	25,000	0.4
Multiple disabilities	106,000	1.8
Deaf-blindness	1,000	0.0
Autism and traumatic brain injury	54,000	0.9
Developmental delay	2,000	0.0
Preschool disabled	564,000	9.6
All disabilities	5,904,000	100.0

Source: U.S. Department of Education, Office of Special Education Programs, Data Analysis System (DANS).

commitment to ensure that all children and youths with disabilities have the right to a free, appropriate public education in the least restrictive environment. The law also requires nondiscriminatory assessment, an individualized educational program (IEP), and the family's right to informed consent and due process. (See Appendix D for a summary of IDEA 1997 regulatory issues.)

The importance of the family's role in providing a special education for a child who has a disability is recognized by the requirement that schools involve a child's family members in the design and delivery of a program tailored to the child. More specifically, federal law requires that parents and school personnel work together to produce a child's individualized education program (IEP); for children birth to 3 years of age, parents must be involved in developing an individualized family service plan (IFSP; IDEA, 1997). The IFSP addresses the accommodations the child will need, and the services the family will need to assist in delivering those accommodations. These services frequently include training to teach specific skills such as living and communication skills, or to reinforce learning at home (Kirk, Gallagher, & Anastasiow, 2003).

This emphasis on the family's involvement reflects the current focus among special educators and service professionals to serve students from an ecological, or interactionist perspective (Bronfenbrenner, 1986). This model reflects a movement from treating the individual who has a disability to treating the social environment in which individuals live and interact, and in which behaviors are affected. For example, helping family members deal with the stresses of living with and caring for a child with special needs will help to maintain a positive home environment that, in turn, will enable all family members to live

Children with special learning needs are entitled to be taught in the "least restrictive environment." Special resource teachers typically assist students being taught in regular classroom settings.

in more relaxed and mutually supportive relationships. Additionally, when community attitudes, practices, and service agencies further support the family in providing for a child with disabilities, the overlapping social spheres of influence in the child's learning (family, school, and community) join together to benefit not only that child but also other family members, the school, and the community (Epstein, 1994; Turnbull & Turnbull, 1997). (See Appendix A for community resource ideas.)

MISCONCEPTIONS ABOUT STUDENTS WITH DISABILITIES, THEIR PARENTS AND FAMILIES

Individuals who require a special education because they have a disability are frequently misunderstood. In some instances they are misunderstood because of the obvious physical or severe nature of their exceptionality which many people use as a reason to exclude them from participating in mainstream activities. Generally, there is sympathy and support shown toward these individuals. Those who have less obvious disabilities (e.g., attention-deficit disorder) may be perceived as quite able and capable of participating in mainstream activities with little or no special consideration. These individuals may receive little understanding and support from the broader community. The parents and family members of individuals with disabilities are also frequently misunderstood because of common perceptions and expectations about the family's role in the treatment and care of family members who are disabled.

Hallahan and Kauffman (2000, pp. 5, 45, 515) discuss the following myths and facts related to individuals with disabilities and their families. An understanding of these myths and facts will help service providers to better understand this special group of students and the concerns and actions of their family members.

Myth: Parents neglect responsibility and "drain the system" to care for and provide special education for their children.

Fact: The vast majority of parents are highly involved in caring for and delivering special services to their children. Federal law requires schools to actively involve parents and other family members in providing special services.

Myth: A disability is a handicap.

Fact: A disability may or may not be a handicap. A disability is an inability to perform a particular function. A handicap is a disadvantage imposed on an individual because of a disability. With proper accommodation, a person with a disability (or handicapping condition) need not be handicapped.

Myth: Public schools are not required to educate children with certain disabilities.

Fact: To receive federal funds, every school system must provide a free, appropriate education for every disabled student regardless of the disabling condition.

Myth: Students with disabilities must be included in standardized testing and follow the same testing routine as students without disabilities.

Fact: Students with disabilities are not automatically excluded from taking standardized tests. While most disabled students are included in standardized testing programs, they may be excluded if a given test is judged inappropriate. Some students may require procedural adaptations to accommodate their specific disabilities.

Myth: Research has established that special (self-contained) classes are ineffective learning structures for disabled students, and that mainstream and inclusion structures are better.

Fact: Research comparing special versus mainstream and inclusion placement models has been inconclusive because of flawed research. Researchers are focusing on finding ways to make all learning structures work more effectively.

Myth: Students with disabilities are excluded from following the same rules of discipline that apply to other students.

Fact: In the majority of cases, the same disciplinary rules apply to students with and without disabilities. However, students with certain disabilities may be removed from a traditional school setting and be taught in an alternative setting.[1]

SERVING THE NEEDS OF STUDENTS WITH DISABILITIES AND THEIR FAMILIES

Although recommended learning accommodations will vary depending upon a child's specific disability, common strategies that accommodate the special education of children with disabilities and the needs of their families are generally recognized. The following insights will help teachers and other service providers understand and better serve the needs of these children and their families.

A general learning characteristic of individuals with a disability is that they require more time to learn and master skills. Also, they function best by participating in structured learning environments characterized by direct instruction, multimodal learning experiences, individual or small-group learning settings, and by being given learning tasks that they are able to complete with high rates of success (DeBoer & Fister, 1995; McLaughlin, 1993; Wood, 1998). Students who have special needs also benefit when classroom transition procedures (moving from one activity to another) are modified to accommodate their special needs. Specific transition accommodations include (a) allowing students extra time to organize materials before changing from one activity to another, (b) assigning a classmate to serve as an "organizational helper," (c) programming students for transitions by giving advanced notice and expectations for the transition, and (d) displaying lists of materials and steps necessary to complete assignments until routines are established (Washington State Department of Public Instruction, 1994). These accommodations help students comply with school rules and expectations and, therefore, enable them to participate more fully in learning opportunities during the instructional day. Helping parents establish similar practices at home will reinforce these organizational patterns that are so important for achieving school success.

Parents and family members of children who have disabilities also have special needs. Parents often react with shock and denial at the suggestion that their child may have a learning problem and qualify for special education services. When a child has a special learning need and it is first brought to the parents' attention, the family usually reacts with shock and denial. They may insist that the teacher just doesn't see their child in the same way that they do. They may accuse the child's previous teachers of not having taught well. The mother may rationalize and say the father has the same problem with reading or spelling that the child does.

---

[1] From D. P. Hallahan and J. M. Kauffman. *Exceptional Learners: Introduction To Special Education,* 8e. Published by Allyn and Bacon, Boston, MA. Copyright © 2000 by Pearson Education. Adapted by permission of the publisher.

After testing confirms that the child is eligible for special services, the parents may need guidance while adjusting to the present and future implications of the child's disability. Parents who are reluctant to accept their child's disability may experience feelings of failure and direct their anger toward the school. Parents may respond to school-initiated contacts about their child's learning disability with defensiveness because they were unaware that the child had a problem or they may have been given ambiguous or misleading information. Communicating with parents of children with learning disabilities can be an emotionally charged experience because they fear for their child's social and academic future.

Parents need reassurance from school personnel that the primary cause of most disabilities is unknown, and that they need to focus their energies on collaborating with others to provide appropriate treatment and accommodations for their child. Parents, and siblings too, must make tremendous adjustments as they learn to accept, cope with, and provide for the needs of the child who has a disability. Siblings may resent the extra attention parents give to the child with special needs. Often, the family's daily routines are interrupted to accommodate the needs of the child with a disability. Frequently, family activities, time, and material resources are compromised to provide necessary services and accommodations. Understandably, these compromises and demands may easily result in high levels of family stress (Dyson, 1997; Gavidia-Payne & Stoneman, 1997). Administrators and teachers who understand the stresses experienced by the family of a child with special needs will want to be sensitive to the family's circumstances by being tolerant and helpful as they work to involve them in their child's education.

By implementing the above recommendations, individuals with disabilities will be spared unnecessary barriers and may be empowered to demonstrate their abilities. When these recommendations are implemented, family members will also be given the support they need to help their family member through the stresses and challenges they must overcome to live full and productive lives.

STUDENTS WHO ARE GIFTED AND TALENTED

Children who are gifted and talented also fall into the category of children who have special learning needs. The current federal definition of gifted and talented students comes from 1993 legislation:

> Gifted and talented children and youth are those with outstanding talent who perform or show the potential for performing at remarkably high levels of accomplishment when compared with others of their age, experience, or environment. These children and youth exhibit high performance capability in intellectual, creative, and or artistic areas, possess an unusual leadership capacity, or excel in specific academic fields. They require services or activities not ordinarily provided by the schools. Outstanding talents are present in children and youth from all cultural groups, across all economic strata, and in all areas of human endeavor. (*U.S. Dept. of Education, Office of Educational Research and Improvement. National Excellence: A Case for Developing America's Talent,* 1993)

All family members must make adjustments to daily activities and routines in order to accomodate the needs of a family member who has special needs. What specific adjustments must the family make? Remember, not all people who have special needs are physically handicapped.

This definition applies to those students who demonstrate exceptional ability or talent in particular areas of development, and who require a special education to accommodate the development of that ability or talent. In addition to mental ability, areas of exceptionality include a series of special abilities. Identified by Howard Gardner (1983, 1999), this series of special abilities, or "multiple intelligences," reflects eight areas of giftedness including linguistic, logical-mathematical, spatial, bodily-kinesthetic, musical, interpersonal, intrapersonal, and naturalist.

Each of Gardner's intelligences enables individuals to perform those tasks that enable them to excel at particular professions. For example, linguistic intelligence enables individuals to use written and oral language skillfully and can be found in successful novelists, poets, and lecturers. Logical-mathematical intelligence enables individuals to use calculation to engage in deductive and inductive reasoning and is characteristic of mathematicians and scientists. Spatial intelligence enables individuals to use notation and spatial configurations and leads them to become skilled architects, sculptors, and mechanics. Bodily-kinesthetic intelligence enables athletes, dancers, and surgeons to perform exact tasks with their bodies. Musical intelligence gives music composers and performers a sensitivity to pitch, rhythm, texture, and timbre. Interpersonal and intrapersonal intelligences give individuals the ability to understand others' actions and motivations and can be found in successful teachers, salespeople, therapists, and politicians. Naturalist intelligence gives individuals the ability to see patterns in nature and understand systems created by humans and nature.

Individuals with this type of intelligence typically do well as farmers, botanists, ecologists, or landscapers (Ramos-Ford & Gardner, 1997; Santrock, 2001).

Unlike those students who have a documented disability, and whose learning needs are protected by federal law, learning accommodations of students who are gifted and talented are not protected by similar legislation (Ford, Russo, & Harris, 1995; Gallagher, 1995; Karnes & Marquardt, 1997). Rather, the federal definition of gifted children and youths is intended to offer guidance to state and district educational agencies to provide appropriate learning opportunities. Because of the vast flexibility afforded states and school districts in accommodating the needs of students who are gifted and talented, a wide variety of programs exist. School districts that focus almost exclusively on these students may do so at the expense of programs to serve students who have exceptional abilities in other areas. Frequently, existing physical education and arts programs serve as the only opportunity students with superior artistic, musical, or athletic abilities have to nurture their giftedness (Meece, 2002). Unfortunately, many school districts eliminate these programs when faced with financial shortfalls.

Additionally, because federal guidelines to protect the special education needs of students who are gifted and talented are lacking, many school divisions may not have early identification programs—a slight especially to those students who come from low-income families or who also may have disabilities (Ford, 1998; Gallagher & Gallagher, 1994). Another area of concern is that students may not be protected from biased screening procedures and cultural stereotypes. For example, whereas girls are overrepresented in elementary

One option for accomodating the learning needs of gifted and talented students is to offer an accelerated curriculum focused on developing problem solving skills. What do you think of this option? Can you suggest other options?

school programs for students who are gifted and talented, in high school and college, girls are significantly outnumbered by boys in science and mathematics courses for students with high ability (Eccles, 1995). Also, a recent study indicated that only 8% of African American students were enrolled in gifted programs, even though they constituted 16% of the public school population (Hallahan & Kauffman, 2000, p. 490). Other groups of students who are gifted and talented who are at risk of receiving special services include those who are underachievers or disabled (Treffinger, 1998; Whitmore, 1986)—a deplorable circumstance given the fact that giftedness is known to occur in combination with all disabling conditions (Sacks, 1995).

MISCONCEPTIONS ABOUT STUDENTS WITH SPECIAL GIFTS OR TALENTS

Students with special abilities are often misunderstood. Unlike students who have a physical or mental disability, those who have special gifts and talents must deliberately foster their giftedness, sometimes at the risk of stigma or rejection. This fact is recognized by Hallahan and Kauffman (2000), who report that "Many people have a low level of tolerance for those who eclipse the ordinary individual in some area of achievement" (p. 468). It is documented in the literature that children with special gifts and talents are commonly victims of criticism or social isolation by other children or their parents (Cross, 1997; Swiatek, 1998).

The following myths and facts relating to students with special gifts or talents will help practitioners better understand this special group of students and the concerns of their family members.

Myth: Those with special intellectual gifts are physically weak, socially incompetent, narrow in interests, and prone to emotional instability.

Fact: Most individuals with special intellectual gifts are healthy, socially attractive, and well adjusted.

Myth: Children with special gifts or talents are usually bored with school and antagonistic toward teachers.

Fact: Most children with special gifts like school and adjust well to their peers and teachers. Some will, however, dislike school and have social or emotional problems.

Myth: Students with special gifts or talents tend to be mentally unstable.

Fact: Those with special gifts or talents are about as likely to be well adjusted and emotionally healthy as those who do not have such gifts.

Myth: Three to five percent of the population have special gifts or talents.

Fact: The percentage of the population that is found to have special gifts or talents depends on the definition of giftedness used. Some definitions include only one or two percent of the population; others, over 20 percent.

Myth: Giftedness is a stable trait, consistent during a person's life.

Fact: For some, special gifts develop early and continue throughout life; for others, talents are not noticed until adulthood. Occasionally, a child who shows outstanding ability becomes a nondescript adult.

Myth: People who have special gifts do everything well.

Fact: Some have superior abilities of many kinds; others have superior talents in only one area.

Myth: A person has special intellectual gifts if he or she scores above a certain level on intelligence tests.

Fact: IQ is only one indication of one kind of giftedness. Creativity and high motivation are also indications of giftedness. Gifts or talents in some areas, such as the visual and performing arts, are not assessed by IQ tests.

Myth: Students who have a true gift or talent for something will excel without special education. They need only the incentives and instruction that are appropriate for all students.

Fact: Some children with special gifts or talents will achieve at high levels without special education, and go on to accomplish great things even when they face great obstacles. But most will not come close to achieving at a level commensurate with their potential unless their talents are deliberately fostered by instruction that is appropriate for their advanced abilities.[2]

SERVING THE NEEDS OF STUDENTS WHO ARE GIFTED AND TALENTED AND THEIR FAMILIES

Whereas program offerings to serve the learning needs of students who are gifted and talented may vary tremendously, the special learning needs of these students are rather consistent. The literature encourages school divisions to provide programs that reflect several accommodations known to benefit the learning needs of these students. These adaptations to the standard curriculum include inclusion or cluster grouping (small groups of students who are gifted placed with typical students), ability grouping, special courses or programs, flexible pacing, student acceleration, content acceleration, content novelty, problem-based learning, and adapting teaching strategies (Kirk, Gallagher, & Anastasiow, 2003, pp. 138–149). Other experts refine these adaptations by suggesting self-directed learning and independent studies related to developing critical thinking skills (Ford, Baytops, & Harmon, 1997; Tarpley, 2000).

Generally, parents of children identified as gifted and talented are actively involved in ensuring that their children receive appropriate learning accommodations. For this reason, teachers and school administrators must frequently interact with parents and family members under rather tense cir-

---

2 From D. P. Hallahan, J. M. Kauffman. *Exceptional Learners: Introduction to Special Education*, 8e. Published by Allyn and Bacon, Boston, MA. Copyright ©2000 by Pearson Education. Adapted by permission of the publisher.

Parents of gifted and talented students are usually quite willing to meet with teachers to discuss their child's academic program. What kind of involvement should teachers expect of the parents of gifted and talented students?

cumstances, especially when parents' demands cannot be satisfied due to program limitations resulting from the financial constraints faced by the school divisions. Even though local school boards will need to address some parental concerns (e.g., funding and program matters), classroom teachers will also be expected to interact and work with parents in a supportive and cooperative manner.

By anticipating the difficulties that may arise when programs for students who are gifted and talented fail to meet parental expectations, school personnel can work to establish a spirit of understanding and cooperation by initiating strategies such as inviting family members to sit on advisory boards, by recruiting family members to share their time and talents to provide enrichment programs, and by involving parents and other family members in recruiting human community resources to provide enrichment programs.

It is important for school administrators and teachers to understand that the parents of these students have a right to advocate for their children's educational programs. School personnel may need to make conscious efforts to appreciate and welcome the involvement efforts of these family members.

CONCLUSION

Students who have special needs are, indeed, special. Parents and family members of children who have a disability or who are gifted and talented are tremendously committed to advocating for and being involved in their children's education. School administrators and teachers need to make conscious efforts to appreciate and welcome the involvement efforts of these families.

APPLICATION

Working with Families

Teachers can be a great source of comfort and support to families with children who have special learning needs. Parents of a child who is gifted or talented may experience frustration because the school lacks the resources to provide challenging instructional programs or enrichment activities. Suggest learning activities that are extensions of the curriculum that parents can do at home with the child at home to stimulate interests and talents. Identify and recommend to parents community resources such as afterschool enrichment programs at youth organizations or churches that children can enjoy and find challenging.

Parents of a child with learning disabilities may experience frustration because they don't know how to help their child. To help parents guide homework sessions, suggest a structured, uncluttered environment that eliminates unnecessary distractions to help the child focus. Remind parents to be supportive without stepping in to finish the homework when the child encounters difficulty. Children with physical disabilities may tire easily and could do better if they worked on their homework in shorter increments of time. Show parents how to develop a behavior chart that has rewards for small accomplishments. For example, if children clean their rooms or complete homework promptly, they will receive a number of stars on the chart. For every five stars, the child will receive a small reward. The reward could be something as simple as letting the child choose a video to watch with the family, or selecting the menu for dinner. The behavior chart can be useful in helping the child learn to set and achieve short-term goals.

Talk to parents about the impact of the child's special learning requirements on other children in the family. It is important for sisters and brothers to understand why the child with special needs may require more attention at times. Encourage parents to set aside time for other children in the family who also have needs. It is important for teachers and parents to establish a good system of two-way communication to maintain regular contact. Decide together whether to call the parents on a weekly basis or to send home brief written reports. Ask parents for suggestions on what works with a particular child. Try to identify the child's strengths and let parents know what the child can do particularly well. It is important to maintain regular contact with the parents. Listen for clues from the parents on what the family likes to do. For example, if family mealtimes are important, suggest that the child participate in preparing the food. Children can learn to read recipes, practice their fractions, organize ingredients into categories, follow a sequence, and think ahead. Encourage parents to talk to their children about what their day was like and to ask them what the best part of the day was, or to share something they thought was funny.

The following case study illustrates the complexities involved in working with students with special needs and their families. The case reflects several issues related to accommodating a gifted child who also has a disability. The case also highlights the importance of good communication among teachers, students, and parents. The names of the characters have been changed, but the situation is based on an actual event. As a teacher, you are likely to encounter similar situations.

Bob and Martha Henderson couldn't believe their eyes. They were shocked at what they saw as they scanned their son's report card that had arrived in that day's mail. The F in the final grade column indicated that John had failed his third year of high school English. A comment printed next to John's grade offered an explanation for the failure. The comment read: "Incomplete after several warnings!" The message was initialed "J.B.," by John's English teacher, Janice Becker. His other grades were good; in addition to the F, he received two A's, a B+, and a B. The Hendersons found it difficult to believe that John had failed English. He had given no indication of the possibility of failing any of his courses when he left home the previous week to work for his Uncle Jerry in Atlanta.

John had always been a precocious child. He was able to read at age 4 and had exceptional verbal skills. From the time he entered kindergarten his advanced language skills had astonished his teachers. Even now in his junior year of high school his remarkable speaking and writing skills impressed his teachers. Mr. Driscoll, the principal of Newport High School, publicly complimented John during a school assembly for having achieved a near-perfect score on the PSAT.

Even though John possessed exceptional language skills, enjoyed writing, and attended class regularly, he had managed to fail English! The Hendersons were perplexed. They appreciated John's academic potential, but they also knew that he could procrastinate. During middle school and his first year in high school, he often had trouble completing assignments. Yet, in more recent years John had made great progress managing his time. To their knowledge he had benefited from treatment for his attention-deficit disorder (ADD), was exercising self-monitoring skills, and had been completing assignments on time. They were proud of the progress John had made in recent years, yet wondered whether his previous procrastination tendencies had resurfaced without their knowledge. They were hoping, however, that the school's reporting system had made an error.

The Hendersons called the school immediately and asked to speak to the principal. Mr. Driscoll also expressed surprise that John had failed English. During their brief conversation it was decided that Mr. Driscoll would ask Ms. Becker for a more detailed explanation and the Hendersons would ask John for his side of the story. They agreed to meet in Mr. Driscoll's office the following Monday to share their findings.

The Hendersons were reluctant to call John with the disappointing news of his failure. They hoped that he would not need to return home to attend summer school. His summer job in Atlanta meant a lot to John. His uncle had invited him to work in the office of his construction company because of his exceptional knowledge of computer technology. John had been so eager to begin work that he left for Atlanta the day school closed for summer vacation.

John was upset to learn that he had failed English. According to John, Ms. Becker had given him the option of writing his semester project on a topic of his choice or on the topic she had assigned to the class. Even though she strongly encouraged him to abandon writing his short story titled "The Foiled Plot Aboard the Staten Island Ferry," she never insisted. John said that he gave Ms. Becker his 40-page short story 2 days before the assignment was due. He also said that Ms. Becker expressed her displeasure at the time, but that he reminded her of their agreement and said it was impossible for him to start over and complete the other writing assignment in just 2 days. John said Ms. Becker was mean to fail him after agreeing with him earlier that her assigned topic was not a topic he wanted to write about, and that he should "think about it." According to John, he thought about it and decided to write his short story.

The Hendersons met with the principal and presented John's side of the story. During the meeting Mr. Driscoll said that he had spoken to Ms. Becker and that her interpretation of conversations with John was quite different from John's. According to Ms. Becker, John protested writing on the assigned topic (a comparison of the love relationship between the central characters in *Romeo and Juliet* and *Our Town*), saying it was stupid and meaningless. She did remember saying to John following his protest, "Well, what assignment would you give if you were the teacher?"

Mr. Driscoll said that Ms. Becker remembered John saying something about a short story, but that she reminded him that the assignment was not intended to be a creative narrative piece. She also recalled that she ended the communication by advising John to "Think about it." Ms. Becker also reported that John never discussed the assignment with her again, even after she reminded him of an upcoming due date for students wishing to submit their rough drafts for her appraisal and comments. According to Ms. Becker, when she reminded John of this option, he responded, "I'm fine."

After Mr. Driscoll related Ms. Becker's account of the story, he sighed and told the Hendersons that, in his judgment, Ms. Becker had been justified in giving John a failing grade. He pointed out that not only had John failed to heed Ms. Becker's directions but he also failed to communicate with her about the progress of his work. Mr. Driscoll added that even though John had made good progress self-monitoring his ADD behavior, he still needed to learn accountability skills to function in the real world.

The Hendersons said they disagreed with Mr. Driscoll's analysis and suggested that, because Ms. Becker had known of John's ADD, she should have taken into account his special need to have expectations and directions clearly stated and understood. They further argued that regardless of the miscommunication, John's short story, combined with his grades during earlier grading periods, surely would have added up to a passing grade for the year. They contended that the failing grade did not reflect an accurate measure of John's academic competence. They expressed their concern that if John had to attend summer school he would be unable to work to earn money for college, which they believed would provide John with a better lesson in learning about the real world than completing a writing assignment on love relationships between four teenage literary figures.

CASE STUDY DISCUSSION GUIDE

Themes: The negative effects of miscommunication; issues related to eligibility; procedures for monitoring exceptional students; curriculum modification; grading and retention issues.

Actors

A. How would you characterize each of the actors in this case? (List each person's name and give one-, two-, or three-word descriptions for each actor.)

Probes

1. How do you think each of the actors in this case feels?
2. What are the effects of this case on the actors? What dilemmas do they face?
3. What does each actor want to achieve? (List what you think each actor wants to happen.)

Issues

B. What are the major issues in this case? (Make a list of these issues.)

Probes

1. What does the term *accommodation* mean when applied to students with special needs? Should the fact that John had ADD make any difference in how Ms. Becker communicated with him? What does the right to "due process" mean when applied to students with special needs? Were John and his parents given due process?
2. Think about grading. What should a grade reflect? Should a student who scores a near-perfect score on the PSAT fail English?
3. Why did the principal not know of John's failure until he was informed by the Hendersons?
4. Should teachers document transactions with students with special needs and their parents? What kinds of documentation should be kept?
5. What rights of "academic freedom" do teachers have?

Problems or Conflicts

What are the major problems or conflicts in this case? Make a list of these problems or conflicts and specify whether you think they stem from personal or institutional origins. Now, examine the list further. Can you separate the items on your list into primary and secondary subcategories? (After completing this last step, you may find it easier to suggest solutions to the problems or conflicts in this case.)

Probes

1. Did John act reasonably? Why or why not?
2. Did Ms. Becker act reasonably? Why or why not?
3. Did Mr. Driscoll act reasonably? Why or why not?

4. Are the Hendersons justified in their analysis of the situation? Why or why not?

5. Were John's legal rights violated?

Solutions

How could the problems or conflicts in this case have been prevented? If you had been one of the actors in this case, what would you have done differently?

Probes

1. What could Ms. Becker have done to make certain John understood her expectations?

2. What could John have done to make sure that he clearly understood the teacher's expectations? What skills would John have needed to do this?

3. What could the Hendersons have done to prevent the primary conflicts in this case?

4. What school procedures could have prevented the primary conflicts in this case?

5. What implications for effective home–school communication and collaboration are suggested by this case?

SUPPLEMENTAL ACTIVITIES

The following activities include two types of field experiences: a school-based activity and a community-based activity. The school activity can be done as you complete your early field experience that requires observations at a school site. The community activity is designed to acquaint you with social service agencies that provide family support and resources. Detailed directions for participant observations during early field experiences are provided in Appendix C.

FIELD EXPERIENCE A

School-Based Activity

Research the guidelines and policies for accommodating the special learning needs of gifted and talented students in two or more school districts. Compare the two programs. How are they different? Discuss these differences with your study group to determine the quality of each program. You may want to direct your inquiry and discussion with the following questions:

1. What guidelines are followed for determining gifted (or talented) status?

2. If academic achievement is a criteria, how is this criteria determined? Is IQ measured on a standardized test? If other or additional (nonstandardized) measures are used, what are they?

3. What percentage of the school population is identified as gifted or talented? Are boys and girls equally represented in these programs?

4. What special programs are made available to students who are gifted or talented? How many students who are being accommodated because they

have a disabling condition also receive accommodation for being gifted or talented?

5. What percentage of students with gifted or talented status are from culturally and linguistically different backgrounds?

6. What is the nature of the learning opportunities made available to students who are gifted or talented? Are students taught in clustered groups in inclusive classrooms? If so, are all students in these classrooms gifted and talented, or are typical students also included? Are students who are gifted or talented taught in a "pull-out" program? If so, what is the nature of this program? How frequently and for how many minutes per week do students participate? Are students who are gifted or talented required to make up academic work missed while participating in the pull-out program? Do these students attend separate schools, or participate in special afterschool, Saturday, or summer programs? If so, describe these programs. Who pays for participation in these programs?

7. Do programs for students who are gifted or talented allow for flexible pacing, acceleration, or curriculum compacting? Describe how any of these accommodations are delivered.

8. Are there special qualifications required of those who teach students who are gifted or talented? What kind of in-service do these teachers receive?

9. How are parents of students who are gifted or talented involved in the program? Does the school or district have a parent advisory committee to help direct the program? If so, what is the membership of this committee? How often does it meet?

Interview two or three teachers of different grade levels about the instructional methods and accommodations they make for students with special needs. Among the students they have taught, how many had exceptional needs, and what were they? What classroom accommodations did they use to teach these children? What resources did they use? Were parents and family members involved? How did they collaborate with parents and family members to deliver services to these children?

FIELD EXPERIENCE B   *Community-Based Activity*

Interview the principal, assistant principal, or guidance counselor and ask for a list of community agencies and other resources available to families and school personnel that serve children with special needs in the community. Visit three or four of these agencies to learn about the particular services they provide and any requirements they may have for delivering these services. Find answers to the following questions:

1. What services are provided?

2. How widely used are the agency's services?

3. How active are local school personnel in recommending or using the agency's services?

4. Who uses the agency's services? What percentage of the agency's services is directed to children who have a disability and their families? What percentage of their service is directed to children who are gifted or talented?

5. What could be done to expand community resources to serve children with special needs and their families?

After gathering information on the above questions, write a summary report of the availability and use of community resources available to children with special needs and their families in the area.

Collect material for a resource file on students with special needs and their parents. Begin this project by contacting your state department of education for lists and manuals explaining services and parental rights. You can also contact national professional and parent organizations for printed material (see the list in Appendix A). Ask to be added to their mailing lists. Share the information you collect with your classmates and colleagues.

RESPONSE JOURNAL PROMPTS

As an alternative to using the **Case Study Discussion Guide,** reflect on the case and construct a written response to the following prompts:

1. Assume the role of each actor in the case. What would you have said or done differently? Why?

2. What role should the school principal play in preparation for or during a teacher–parent conference?

ROLE PLAYING AND REFLECTION EXERCISE

Together with a classmate, role-play a scenario depicting a dialogue between the teacher and parent of a child suspected of having a disability. Assume one of the following roles:

- Teacher who thinks the child may have a disability because of the child's low achievement
- Parent who disagrees with the teacher and suggests that the teacher change instructional strategies
- Parent who thinks the child may have a disability because of the child's low achievement
- Teacher who disagrees with the parent and suggests that the child lacks responsible behavior and doesn't apply himself[3]

DISCUSSION

Following the role play, discuss the conflicting positions. During the discussion, construct lists of the strong and weak arguments of each player, then decide how the conflict depicted in this scenario could be resolved.

---

[3] This scenario could also focus on opposing views regarding a student's eligibility for inclusion in the school's program for students who are gifted or talented.

IMPLICATIONS FOR FAMILY INVOLVEMENT

Following the role-play activity, identify the "do's" and "don't's" of teacher behavior when (a) initiating interaction with parents about sensitive issues, and (b) interacting with parents who have conflicting views about the teaching or treatment of their child.

REFERENCES

Bronfenbrenner, U. (1986). Ecology of the family as a context for human development: Research perspectives. *Developmental Psychology, 22*(6), 723–742.

Cross, T. L. (1997). Psychological and social aspects of educating gifted students. *Peabody Journal of Education, 72* (3&4) 180–200.

DeBoer, A., & Fister, S. (1995). *Working together: Tools for collaborative teaching.* Longmont, CO: Sopris West.

Dyson, L. L. (1997). Fathers and mothers of school-age children with developmental disabilities: Parental stress, family functioning, and social support. *American Journal on Mental Retardation, 102,* 267–279.

Eccles, J. S. (1995). Why doesn't Jane run? Sex differences in educational and occupational patterns. In F. D. Horowitz & M. O'Brien (Eds.), *The gifted and talented: Developmental perspectives.* Washington, DC: American Psychological Association.

Education for All Handicapped Children Act. (1975). (P. L. 94–142) 20 U.S.C. §§ 1400 *et seq.* Renamed Individuals with Disabilities Education Act, 1997. P. L. 99–457, P. L. 100–630, & P. L. 100–476, 20 U.S.C., §§ 1400–1485.

Epstein, J. I. (1994). Theory to practice: School and family partnerships lead to school improvement and student access. In C. I. Fagnano & B. Z. Werber (Eds.), *School, family, and community interaction: A view from the firing lines* (p.41). Boulder, CO: Westview Press.

Ford, D. Y. (1998). The under-representation of minority students in gifted education: Problems and promises in recruitment and retention. *Journal of Special Education, 32,* 4–14.

Ford, D. Y., Baytops, J. L., & Harmon, D. A. (1997). Helping gifted minority students reach their potential: Recommendations for change. *Peabody Journal of Education, 72*(3&4), 201–216.

Ford, D. Y., Russo, C. J., & Harris, J. J., III. (1995). Meeting the educational needs of the gifted: A legal imperative. *Roeper Review, 17,* 224–231.

Gallagher, J. J. (1995). Education of gifted students. A civil rights issue? *Phi Delta Kappan, 76,* 408–410.

Gallagher, J. J. & Gallagher, S. (1994). *Teaching the gifted child* (4th ed.). Boston: Allyn & Bacon.

Gardner, H. (1983). *Frames of mind: The theory of multiple intelligences.* New York: Basic Books.

Gardner, H. (1999). *Intelligence reframed: Multiple intelligences for the 21st century.* New York: Basic Books.

Gavidia-Payne, S., & Stoneman, Z. (1997). Family predictors of maternal and paternal involvement in programs for young children with disabilities. *Child Development, 68,* 701–717.

Hallahan, D. P., & Kauffman, J. M. (2000). *Exceptional learners: Introduction to special education* (8th ed.). Boston: Allyn & Bacon.

Individuals with Disabilities Education Act. (1990) P. L. 101–476, 20 U.S.C. §§ 1400 *et seq.*

Individuals with Disabilities Education Act. (1997). P. L. 105–17, 20 U.S.C. §§ 1400 *et seq.*

Karnes, F. A., & Marquardt, R. G. (1997). The fragmented framework of legal protection for the gifted. *Peabody Journal of Education, 72*(3&4), 166–179.

Kirk, S. A., Gallagher, J. J., & Anastasiow, N. J. (2003). *Educating exceptional children.* Boston: Houghton Mifflin.

McLaughlin, V. L. (1993). Curriculum adaptation and development. In B. S. Billingsley (Ed.), *Program leadership for serving students with disabilities.* Richmond, VA: Virginia Department of Education.

Meece, J. L. (2002). *Child & adolescent development for educators* (2nd ed.). Boston: McGraw-Hill.

National excellence: A case for developing America's talent. (1993). Washington, DC: U.S. Department of Education, Office of Educational Research and Improvement.

Ramos-Ford, H., & Gardner, H. (1997). Giftedness from a multiple intelligences perspective. In N. Colangelo & G. Davis (Eds.), *Handbook of gifted education.* Boston: Allyn & Bacon.

Sacks, O. (1995). *An anthropologist on Mars: Seven paradoxical tales.* New York: Knopf.

Santrock, J. W. (2001). Child development (9th ed.) Boston: McGraw-Hill.

Selections from the writings of 'Abdu'l-Bahá. (1997). Wilmette, IL: Bahá Publishing Trust, p. 291.

Swiatek, M. A. (1998). Helping gifted adolescents cope with social stigma. *Gifted Child Today, 21*(1), 42–46.

Tarpley, P. L. (2000). Suggestions for teaching students who are gifted and talented in general education classrooms. In Daniel P. Hallahan & James M. Kauffman, *Exceptional learners: Introduction to special education,* (8th ed., pp. 505–508). Boston: Allyn & Bacon.

Treffinger, D. J. (1998). From gifted education to programming for talent development. *Phi Delta Kappan, 79,* 752–755.

Turnbull, A. P. & Turnbull, H. R. (1997). *Families, professionals, and exceptionality: A special partnership* (3rd ed.). Upper Saddle River, NJ: Merrill/Prentice Hall.

U.S. Department of Education. (1999). *Twenty-First Annual Report to Congress on Implementation of the Individuals with Disabilities Education Act.* Washington, DC: U.S. Department of Education, Office of Special Education Programs.

U.S. Department of Education. (2000) *Twenty-Second Annual Report to Congress on Implementation of the Individuals with Disabilities Education Act.* Washington, DC: U.S. Department of Education, Office of Special Education Programs.

Washington State Department of Public Instruction. (1994). In J. L. Meece (Ed.), *Child & adolescent development for educators* (2nd ed., p. 368). Boston: McGraw-Hill.

Whitmore, J. (1986). Understanding a lack of motivation to excel. *Gifted Child Quarterly, 30,* 66–69.

Wood, J. W. (1998). *Adapting instruction to accommodate students in inclusive settings* (3rd ed.). Upper Saddle, NJ: Merrill/Prentice Hall.

7

HOW TO INVOLVE FAMILIES AND MAINTAIN EFFECTIVE HOME–SCHOOL PARTNERSHIPS

Schools that are most successful in engaging parents and other family members in support of their children's learning look beyond traditional definitions of parent involvement.

—RMC Research Corporation-Denver, a partner in the STAR Center, Region VIII Comprehensive Center, funded by the U.S. Department of Education, April 2000. Reprinted with permission.

Previous chapters treated the differences and complexities characteristic of the contemporary family. Now we turn our attention to the question of how to use this information to involve families and community members. This chapter addresses this important question by examining (1) the nature of effective home–school partnerships, and (2) optional ways that school personnel, family members, and members of the broader community can work together as partners to serve the learning needs of children and youth.

THE NATURE OF EFFECTIVE HOME–SCHOOL PARTNERSHIPS

What are the conditions that bring school personnel and family members together to improve learning opportunities and student achievement? Why do some schools have high levels of involvement, whereas personnel in other schools complain that parents are apathetic and disinterested? What factors account for these differences?

PLANNING FOR INVOLVEMENT

There is overwhelming agreement among experts that the first and most important step in establishing effective home–school partnerships is for school personnel to decide whether they want to involve families in their programs. The next step is to commit themselves to doing whatever it takes to achieve that involvement (Batey, 1996). Epstein, a leading expert in the field of family involvement, reminds school personnel who are serious about wanting high levels of involvement, that developing a comprehensive family involvement program will enable them to achieve their goal. Epstein, Coates, Salinas, Sanders, and Simon (1997) recommend five steps in the development of this comprehensive plan, the first of which is to **form a School Action Team** consisting of administrators, teachers, school staff, parents, students, and community leaders. The mission of this School Action Team is to guide the development of the school's involvement program and integrate it into the school's goals. The second step of Epstein and colleagues' plan is to **locate funding sources** to enable the team to do its work. A number of federal, state, or local funding sources support family involvement. Funds can be used to support demonstration programs, staff development, and coordinators. The third step in the plan is for the team to **assess the school's current practices and needs** to determine a starting point. To do this, the Team is encouraged to look at *present strengths* (Which types of involvement practices are already in place, and for whom?); *family needs* (Are the needs of currently involved families being met, and who are the "hard-to-reach" families, and their needs?); *needed changes* (Which current practices should be changed, and what new practices should be added to serve specific involvement needs?); *expectations* (What do school personnel, family members, and community members expect from each involvement program?); and *links to goals* (How are students performing on indicators of academic achievement?). The fourth step of Epstein and colleagues is to **develop a three-year plan** based on the assessment findings. The plan, which should be shared with all stakeholders, outlines specific steps for implementation and a timeline. The final step is to **identify strategies for monitoring and maintaining implementation** of the various programs. School personnel who are serious about involving families will profit from following this five-step plan; it is a prerequisite to success.

Schools that have successfully implemented partnership programs have provided positive examples for education researchers and technical assistance providers to share in their work with low-performing schools. From 1986 to 1989, the Southwest Educational Development Laboratory analyzed successful schools and identified characteristics of "promising parent involvement programs." According to its findings, successful parent involvement programs have seven elements in common (SERVE, n.d.): written policies, administrative support, training, a partnership approach, networking, evaluation, and two-way communication. These elements are discussed in more detail in the following paragraphs.[1]

WRITTEN POLICIES

Schools that have developed a written policy statement about family involvement are in a better position to work toward achieving successful partnerships. Some home, school, and community partnerships develop a "learning compact" that outlines the goals, expectations, and responsibilities of all partners. This written commitment encourages all partners to share in the responsibility

---

[1]The discussion in this section is based on J. L. Epstein, L. Coates, K. C. Salinas, M. G. Sanders, and B. S. Simon. *School, Family, and Community Partnerships: Your Handbook for Action.* Copyright © 1997 by Corwin Press. Used by permission of Corwin Press, Inc.

of educating children. The National Coalition for Parent Involvement in Education (NCPIE) recommends that policy statements include programs for the families of all students, levels of participation of family members, regular information for families, professional development for teachers, and linkages with social service agencies (SERVE, n.d.).

ADMINISTRATIVE SUPPORT

Successful programs have strong administrative leadership and support. Administrators recruit family and community partners, create a climate for welcoming and listening to all viewpoints, lead partners to work in a collaborative spirit to achieve program goals, provide necessary resources, and work to sustain the motivation of partners.

TRAINING

It is essential that school staff have an understanding of family profiles and the complexities of family life characteristic of the school's population. With this understanding, personnel are able to initiate programs that meet the involvement needs of families. Some schools find it helpful to train staff members to recognize personal biases in order to be more responsive to the needs of a variety of family structures and profiles.

PARTNERSHIP APPROACH

Family involvement programs have a sound support base when all stakeholders are involved in assessing needs and designing the program. Achieving this support requires hours of recruiting, meeting, and planning, but once done, allows all participants to "buy in" to the program and support its implementation.

NETWORKING

An important component of successful involvement programs is that of networking; that is, communicating with staff from other schools who are implementing involvement programs, sharing ideas and resources.

EVALUATION

When involvement programs include an ongoing monitoring component, adjustments can be made as needs arise. Even with comprehensive and thoughtful planning, activities may often fall short of meeting intended goals. By monitoring program activities, interventions can be made to ensure success.

IMPORTANCE OF TWO-WAY COMMUNICATION

The above features of successful involvement programs recognize that parent involvement means much more than listening to school personnel as they list ways that parents can support teachers' efforts, and complying with these expectations. Rather, effective programs invite two-way communication between home and school so that families and schools are active partners in the education of children and youth. Communication with families should be frequent, clear, easily understood, and in the language spoken in the home. School personnel who approach family members with the attitude that each has an important voice to be heard, take the first and most important step in establishing a viable partnership (Laboratory for Student Success, 1997a).

Typically, teachers and other school personnel who are sensitive to the complex structures, customs, and needs characteristic of contemporary families will make a conscious effort to establish a climate of mutual respect (Canter & Canter, 1991). These teachers recognize that parents are able to provide important information about their child that will help in meeting individual children's needs. For example, some children may have interactive skills that are not displayed at school, or interests and skills not readily observed in the classroom. Teachers may use this knowledge to better relate to these children and more accurately engage them in learning activities. With knowledge of the family, teachers will be able to more appropriately communicate to parents their expectations of how the family can assist their child's learning at home. When school personnel and family members listen to one another, they establish rapport and bonds of mutual trust and cooperation, the foundation upon which, as Hanhan (1998) suggests in "Who's Talking?", effective partnerships are built.

The Laboratory for Student Success, one of the 10 regional educational laboratories funded by the U.S. Department of Education, suggests that teachers can establish positive two-way communication by sending home a weekly or biweekly newsletter, developing a parent feedback form, recognizing acade-

PTA meetings, structured to get parents talking with other parents and school personnel about school issues and concerns, sends a clear message to parents that they are valued members of the school community.

mic and behavioral achievement, organizing a "telephone tree" for the families of students, and communicating personally with parents at least once a month (Laboratory for Student Success, 1997b).

PARENT CONFERENCES, FIRST IMPRESSIONS, AND RAPPORT

The most common form of parent involvement is participation in the parent–teacher conference. It is important for teachers to communicate a welcoming attitude and establish a positive rapport during the initial conference. Creating a positive first impression will put parents at ease and lay a firm foundation for subsequent teacher–parent communication and collaboration. To establish rapport during the initial conference, teachers are encouraged to let parents do much of the talking while they listen to what they have to say on issues related to their child's school success.

The Laboratory for Student Success (1997a) suggests important topics to cover during the initial conference, such as parents' views of their child's strengths and weaknesses, expectations for their child, the nature and extent of their involvement in their child's learning, and unique characteristics of their home. Teachers might ask parents which academic area their child likes most and which he or she tends to avoid, their goals for their child, how they (or other family members) routinely help their child with homework, and their family routine at home before and after school.

When parents are asked these questions, they feel included in their child's schooling, and begin to establish a school partnership with the teacher. Information gleaned from parents' responses to these questions will help the teacher learn about the child's interests, the home environment, and the dynamics of the family—important information that enables the teacher to work successfully with the student and parents during the school year.

INVOLVEMENT OPPORTUNITIES FOR HOME-SCHOOL PARTNERSHIPS

In what ways can school personnel and family members work together to benefit student learning? Whereas the monthly PTA meeting or newsletter may satisfy the needs of some families, they will not serve the needs of most. What kinds of involvement programs should be made available to meet the needs of the various family structures and profiles characteristic of the contemporary family? To answer these questions, we again turn to those schools whose involvement programs have successfully served the needs of their families.

The Region VIII Comprehensive Center, one of 15 organizations funded by the U.S. Department of Education to provide technical assistance to schools, developed a training program to help school personnel establish viable home–school partnerships. This training program, titled *Creating Family Friendly Schools* (STAR Center, 2000a), features cases of schools representing various demographics that have established successful involvement programs to address their unique needs. Profiles of these schools and the successful involvement practices they initiated are presented here because they reflect how, as a result of their creative planning and steadfast commitment, they were able to offer a variety of involvement options. A profile of each of these schools is followed by a sampling of the collective programs they initiated to (1) break down barriers to family involvement, (2) provide information and training to parents and school staff, (3) restructure their schools to support family involvement, (4) bridge school–family differences, and (5) tap community supports for school–family partnerships. Complete descriptions of these case reports are available from RMC Research, Writer's Square Suite 540, 1512 Larimer St., Denver, CO 80202. Ask for *Creating Family Friendly Schools: A Guidebook for Trainers,* Module 5. These cases are reprinted with permission from RMC Research Corporation-Denver, a partner in the STAR Center, Region VIII Comprehensive Center, funded by the U.S. Department of Education.

SCHOOL PROFILES

A Rural Setting: Profile of Atenville Elementary School, Harts, West Virginia

Atenville Elementary School is located in a rural, coal-mining community in West Virginia. Families in the community struggle from geographic isolation, high unemployment, and chronic poverty. All 213 students in grades pre-K–6 at Atenville are white. Many families receive Aid to Families with Dependent Children, and approximately 83% of the school's population receives either free or reduced-price lunch. Many households lack telephones and access to transportation.

Looking for ways to improve home–school communication and increased opportunities for family involvement, Atenville's administration, in partnership with the Parent-Teacher Action Research project at the Institute for Responsive Education (IRE) in Boston, Massachusetts, established the Parents as Educational Partners (PEP) Program during the 1992 school year. Funded primarily through Title I, Goals 2000, and IRE, the program grew by 1996 to include a variety of activities designed to improve communication with families, encourage parent involvement in the classroom, increase parent leadership and decision-making at school, support learning at home, improve parenting skills, and tap community resources. The program also coordinated access to various health and social services available through local and national organizations. The PEP program was credited with increasing student achievement, attendance, discipline, self-esteem, community well-being and community pride (STAR, 2000b).

BREAKING DOWN BARRIERS TO FAMILY INVOLVEMENT
The school initiated the following activities to help break down existing barriers to involvement and prepare the foundation for a school-wide involvement program launched during the 1996–1997 school year: a "telephone tree" staffed by volunteers; a home visitation program participated in by principal, teachers, and trained parent volunteers; a Family Resource Center; and an employed parent coordinator.

OVERCOMING TIME AND RESOURCE CONSTRAINTS

To overcome time and resource constraints, the program focused on hard-to-reach parents. Parent volunteers distributed information about school programs by mail and word of mouth. Volunteers transported families who lacked transportation. The principal and teachers visited the homes of students whose parents had difficulty getting to the school. The principal substitutes in the teachers' classrooms to allow them to make home visits during the school day. The parent coordinator and telephone tree parents conducted home visits to families that were not actively involved and whose children were having difficulties in the classroom. To make it easier for teachers to communicate with parents, the school installed telephones in the classrooms, designated time for daily planning, and provided teachers with duty-free lunch periods.

PROVIDING INFORMATION AND TRAINING TO PARENTS AND SCHOOL STAFF

Programs were supported through information and training that focused on two-way communication. The principal provided training on telephone courtesy and matters of confidentiality to telephone tree parents. The telephone tree parents called 20 to 25 homes at the end of each month to inform parents about school activities during the coming month and to receive feedback on the previous month's programs. They also solicited ideas and suggestions for future activities and services.

Many teachers visit the homes of their students, especially if parents are unable to visit the school. What messages do teachers send to parents when they take the time to make a home visit?

To support learning at home, a local high school teacher conducted math workshops for parents to teach skills needed to help their children with homework. The principal and teachers also offered parent workshops on how to increase the language development of young children, how to support reading, how to increase self-esteem, and how to help with homework.

Parents and other family members (8 per day) were recruited to supervise children in the library, during lunch, and recess. The school provided ongoing training for volunteers on school policies, discipline, confidentiality, and classroom assistance. Training was also provided to members of the school improvement council and the parent involvement team.

RESTRUCTURING SCHOOLS TO SUPPORT FAMILY INVOLVEMENT

The school restructured itself to support family involvement. There was a commitment on the part of school staff and community to improve student achievement by restructuring the school to support successful school–family partnerships.

The school conducted focus groups to assess family needs. Data were used to direct restructuring to meet identified needs. For example, the school introduced block scheduling for students in grades 4 to 6 at the request of parents to ease student transition to the middle school.

A Family Resource Center was established to house parent resources, a teacher workroom, a conference facility, and an informal lounge for volunteers, parents, and teachers. Families participated on all school committees (e.g., the involvement team, action research team, school improvement council, and Title I schoolwide planning team).

BRIDGING SCHOOL–FAMILY DIFFERENCES

The parent programs were focused on building comfort and trust between school and home to help parents overcome their own negative school experiences. There were school-sponsored GED and other adult education classes taught at the school during evenings and on Saturday mornings with child care made available.

The programs encouraged and supported frequent teacher–family contact by phone and/or home visitation. Family members were invited to assist in classrooms, the office, and the library.

TAPPING EXTERNAL SUPPORTS FOR SCHOOL–FAMILY PARTNERSHIPS

The school tapped external support to facilitate school–family partnerships. For-credit courses were offered to parents at the school, in collaboration with Southern West Virginia Community College (Atenville teachers who taught these courses received stipends from the community college).

Monthly donations from Children, Inc.—based in Richmond, Virginia—provided the school with clothing and other goods to be distributed to needy families. A partnership with Youth Works, based in Minneapolis, Minnesota, provided 60 to 70 youth volunteers each summer to work with families and tutor children. A pediatric mobile unit provided by the West Virginia Children's

Health Project visited the school weekly to provide health-care services to children. The school's Family Center made appointments and served as the waiting room. A local dentist provided yearly dental screening at the school on a volunteer basis. A Community library was established with Goals 2000 funds.

EVIDENCE OF SUCCESS

How successful was the program? During the 1992 school year parents volunteered 2,000 hours of service at the school. In 1996 the number of volunteer hours had increased to more than 7,000 hours. Almost half of the families at the school participated in volunteer training during the 1995–1996 school year. The number of sixth graders who believed they would graduate from high school and attend college grew from 72% to 79% between 1992 and 1995.

The number of students participating in an after-school tutoring program increased from 21 to 62 over a three-year period. Between 1992 and 1996 student achievement scores of third and sixth graders on the Comprehensive Test of Basic Skills (CTBS) increased from the 58th and 59th percentiles, respectively, to the 71st and 63rd percentiles. Student suspensions decreased from 12 in 1991 to an average of 3 per year through 1996.

An Inner-City Setting: Profile of Roosevelt High School, Dallas, Texas

In 1992 fewer than one quarter of Roosevelt High School students met minimum academic standards on the Texas Assessment of Academic Skills (TAAS). The Texas Education Agency (TEA) placed Roosevelt on its list of low-performing schools, and the Dallas Independent School District considered closing the school. At Roosevelt High, 99% of the students are from minority families, and nearly 80% of students are eligible for free or reduced-price lunches. The school also reported that student discipline was a problem, and little or no parent involvement. To address its many problems, the school's leadership decided to join the Alliance Schools Initiative, a partnership between the Texas Interfaith Education Fund (TIEF) and the Texas Education Agency aimed at helping schools develop strong community-based support to increase student achievement in low-income areas.

BREAKING DOWN BARRIERS TO FAMILY INVOLVEMENT

The principal organized a School Improvement Team of school personnel, parents, students, community leaders, and business representatives to plan and direct the school's reform effort. To break down barriers to family involvement, School Improvement Team identified factors that inhibited parent involvement at Roosevelt (e.g., teachers' lack of skills and resources for reaching out to parents of older students, low expectations for family involvement, and the negative attitude of parents regarding their role in the education of their adolescent. The School Improvement Team also identified related factors that discouraged family involvement (e.g., rapid social and economic decay of the surrounding community, the high numbers of single parents working long hours, high numbers of parents who harbored personal negative school experiences, and perception that the only involved parents were those of high-achieving students).

OVERCOMING TIME AND RESOURCE CONSTRAINTS

As a first step to reaching out to *all* parents and improving communication, school staff and community leaders hand-delivered report cards to parents of every student who had one or more failing grades. The group established a procedure for teachers to document the content of consultations with parents (including any agreed-upon course of action) prior to failing a student or placing him or her on academic probation.

The school employed a parent liaison to make an average of 30 to 60 phone calls daily to notify parents and family members of school activities and school board and city council meetings. The liaison also discussed children's disciplinary standing with their family. To address safety concerns, groups of parents were recruited to provide informal security patrols to monitor the school and campus.

PROVIDING INFORMATION AND TRAINING TO PARENTS AND SCHOOL STAFF

Strategic, targeted training, delivered by the Alliance Schools Initiative (ASI), was initiated for teachers, administrators, parents, and community leaders. Parents participated in evening training sessions to acquaint them with what students were expected to know to pass the TAAS test, and how performance on the TAAS might affect their academic futures. Free self-help courses were offered on topics requested by parents (adult literacy, computer literacy, English as a second language, and parenting skills). These courses were developed and taught twice a week by a core group of teachers from Roosevelt.

Parents received instruction in helping their children gain access to college, including how to fill out forms and collect important pieces of documentation.

RESTRUCTURING SCHOOLS TO SUPPORT FAMILY INVOLVEMENT

As an Alliance school, Roosevelt began the process of working to improve student achievement by identifying leaders; the key concerns of parents, staff, and the community; and organizing structures to achieve needed areas of reform. Four "core teams" of teachers, parents, and community members met regularly to monitor program goals. During the 1995–1996 academic year, Roosevelt implemented a school–parent compact that parents, teachers, and students signed annually. The compact included agreements that the school would provide homework assignments that enhanced classroom learning, opportunities for parents to participate in decisions affecting their children, and flexible scheduling of parent meetings and school functions. Parents agreed to maintain communication with the school through conferences and school visits, and to involve themselves in their child's education by supporting the school's programs and expectations for student success.

When school personnel are serious about involving parents, they provide the support they need to become effective home–school partners. A variety of scheduling and site options will enable greater participation.

TAPPING EXTERNAL SUPPORTS FOR SCHOOL–FAMILY PARTNERSHIPS

Resources from the Investment Capital Fund grant (from TEA) enabled "vertical alignments" with feeder schools that emphasized the importance of strengthening academic skills and family involvement. Title I funds helped to support parent involvement activities. Roosevelt received an initial Investment Capital Fund grant of $15,000. The school also received a $59,000 award from the school district for improving attendance by more than 11%. Pepsi-Cola Company awarded the school a $6,000 grant.

EVIDENCE OF SUCCESS

How successful was this school in increasing family involvement and student achievement? Because of achievement gains, Roosevelt was removed from TEA's list of low-performing schools. Between 1992–1993 and 1995–1996, reading scores rose from the 40th percentile to the 81st percentile, math scores rose from the 16th percentile to the 70th percentile, and writing scores rose from the 58th percentile to the 80th percentile.

Attendance jumped 11% between 1992 and 1996. On average, 40 parents participated weekly in the four adult education classes. In 1994, ten parents attended the first PTA meeting, and more than 200 attended the first PTA meeting in 1996. Roughly 80% of parents of sophomores and seniors who had not passed the TAAS attended TAAS training classes in 1996. More than 100 parents, teachers, school administrators, and community members participated in an annual "neighborhood walk" to survey community needs.

An Urban Setting: Profile of Cane Run Elementary School, Louisville, Kentucky

Cane Run Elementary School in Louisville, Kentucky, is located in an urban community. The school is part of the Jefferson County Public School District, one of the 25 largest school districts in the United States. The school's K–5 population of 450 students is 50% African American and 50% White. Approximately 80% of students at Cane Run Elementary are eligible for free or reduced-price lunches. Wanting to increase both parent involvement and options for participation, the staff at Cane Run Elementary School obtained funds available through the 1990 Kentucky Education Reform Act (KERA) to meet their goals.

As a first step to improving the school's involvement program, a Family Resource Center was established. Directed by an advisory council, the Center served the families of all students, as well as members of the surrounding community. A full-time coordinator helped families gain access to school and local community resources.

BREAKING DOWN BARRIERS TO FAMILY INVOLVEMENT

To break down barriers to family involvement, the school formed the Family Resource Advisory Council (FRAC) to direct the Family Resource Center. A full-time staff member was hired to coordinate family involvement activities and help parents gain access to school and community services (e.g., health counseling, medical and social services, transportation to school activities, and student tutoring). An after-school program was established from 3:30 to 6:00 p.m.; the fee of $10.00 per week to participate in the after-school program was waived for families unable to pay in exchange for volunteering their time at school or in the Center.

The school established a Jump Start program for 40 three- and four-year-olds; morning and afternoon sessions were held Monday through Thursday, and on Friday Jump Start staff made home visits to participating families.

Parent meetings were held outside the school building or after business hours to accommodate the schedules of working parents. If impromptu parent conferences were required during the school day, teachers "covered for one another." Parents and family members who were unable to leave their homes were given work to do at home (constructing learning activities, etc.) as a way to support classroom teachers. An "around the clock" answering service was installed so that parents could leave messages at their convenience.

Teachers had access to numerous phones throughout the school. Lists of students' names and phone numbers were located next to all phones (PTA room, library, staff workroom, computer lab, and conference room).

PROVIDING INFORMATION AND TRAINING
TO PARENTS AND SCHOOL STAFF

Family Technology Nights (five times per year) provided training in using computers and families could check out laptops with instructional software to help involve them in their children's education. Family members received training to learn skills and strategies for helping with homework assignments. Workshops were offered to family members to help them learn how to prepare their children for testing. These workshops were held in the evenings, with dinner and child care provided.

Every year the principal, teachers, school staff, and eight parents attended an out-of-town retreat. The retreat offered workshops on best practices, classroom- and home-based learning activities, and addressed a variety of educational issues. The retreat provided an opportunity for administrators, teachers, and parents to dialogue about ways to improve the school's instructional and family involvement programs.

RESTRUCTURING SCHOOLS TO SUPPORT FAMILY INVOLVEMENT

The school empowered parents to make decisions by participating in the school's site-based, decision-making council. The twelve-member council, which included four parents, five teachers, two staff members, and the principal, made decisions regulating approximately 90% of the school's daily operation.

Adjustments were made during student drop-off and pick-up times to enable PTA members an opportunity to speak to and build rapport with hard-to-reach and/or uninvolved parents. PTA members were actively involved in speaking to community agencies and groups to solicit support for school functions and activities.

BRIDGING SCHOOL–FAMILY DIFFERENCES

The school focused on bridging school–family differences through Even Start programs. The Even Start Family Literacy program helped parents develop skills

It is becoming more and more common for schools to have a school council that meets regularly with school administrators to direct the school's daily operation. School councils generally consist of parents, teachers, and staff members. Some school councils also include representatives from the business community. What are the advantages of establishing a school council?

to support learning at home. The school established an on-site early childhood center. Staff in the Even Start program conducted an infant and toddler nursery in the school and offered classes in parenting skills. They also conducted regular visits to the homes of preschool children.

TAPPING EXTERNAL SUPPORTS FOR SCHOOL–FAMILY PARTNERSHIPS
The Kentucky Education Reform Act (KERA) and Title I funds were the primary funding resources for improving family involvement at Cane Run Elementary School. A primary function of the Family Resource Center were to help families gain access to community services and agencies (e.g., mental health counseling, medical services, social services, etc.)

EVIDENCE OF SUCCESS
How successful was this school? Over a ten-year period, PTA membership grew from 60 parents to more than 700 parents and community members. The PTA received over 30 awards for exemplary attendance. In 1995 the school won the state PTA's highest award for local involvement.

An average of four volunteers worked daily in the Family Resource Center. An average of 30 parents visited the school daily to volunteer services. During the five previous years, the average was near zero.

The principal reported steady, though modest, improvement in math and reading scores. Attendance was steady over several years at 94%. Disciplinary referrals decreased by 30% each year.

A Small-Town Setting: Profile of Rodney B. Cox Elementary School, Dade City, Florida

Rodney B. Cox Elementary School is a full-service school located in a semi-rural, small town about 30 miles north of Tampa, Florida. The school serves 512 students in grades pre-K–5, many of whom are the second or third generation in their family to have attended the school. Ninety-three percent of students at Cox are eligible for free or reduced-price lunches. The school has a 21% migrant population, and a mobility rate among students of 56%. Migrant families arrive in mid-October to work in the fruit and vegetable fields, and leave by mid-April. The student population at Cox is 40% African American, 44% Hispanic (many have limited English proficiency), and 16% White. About 20% of Cox students live in households without a telephone, and many families have no car. All students live approximately two miles from the school, and most live in low-income housing units.

BREAKING DOWN BARRIERS TO FAMILY INVOLVEMENT
Like the schools described in the other case studies, teachers and other staff members conducted regular home visits to communicate with parents to break down barriers to family involvement. Though teachers were required to visit students' homes quarterly, most exceeded this requirement. A full-time parent

involvement coordinator and a migrant recruiter made frequent home visits, recruited family members for school committees, and drove parents to ensure their presence at conferences, IEP meetings, or medical referrals arranged by the school's staff.

Activities frequently included meals and child care as an attraction to attend school programs; family members received free lunch when they volunteered during the school day (paid for by fund-raising and vending profits). Teachers encouraged parents to drop in throughout the school day. The principal arranged to cover classes if an emergency parent conference became necessary during the school day.

PROVIDING INFORMATION AND TRAINING TO PARENTS AND SCHOOL STAFF

The school established monthly events to train parents to support learning at home, including "make and take" programs and various workshops scheduled during both evening and afternoon hours to accommodate parents' work schedules. Committees of teachers and parents selected program topics.

Bilingual teachers attended monthly training and/or enrichment events to translate for Spanish-speaking family members. Free adult education classes were offered at the school twice weekly to help parents and other family members acquire skills to assist their children with academics and provide them an opportunity to interact with teachers and school staff.

Teachers attended a three-day summer workshop (Parents Exploring Teaching and Learning Styles) on different learning styles and preferences of students. The parent involvement coordinator took pictures each week of paraprofessionals, parents, and teachers interacting with students for publication in the local newspaper. Descriptions of these photos informed the broader community of ways to become involved in the school.

RESTRUCTURING SCHOOLS TO SUPPORT FAMILY INVOLVEMENT

How did the school restructure to support family involvement? The school provides dental care, counseling, and health care to students and their families through the parent involvement office. The School Advisory Council (SAC) (composed of the principal, teachers, parents, and community members) regularly surveyed all parents and school staff to identify needs. Changes made as a result of survey results included offering parents computer training, publishing a monthly newsletter in English and Spanish, sending daily communication folders home, installing an outdoor sign, and using the local television station to advertise involvement events.

The local business community was organized to sponsor Career Clubs through which students could learn about potential careers. The school employed a certified teacher as a full-time parent involvement coordinator (with no teaching responsibilities); in addition to responsibilities mentioned earlier, the parent involvement coordinator accompanied teachers on home visits if requested.

Members of the business community and community support agencies are valuable human resources who can work with school personnel to help serve a variety of student needs. Serving as a student mentor is one important role that members of the community can be recruited and trained to fill.

The school established a school–parent compact listing goals for students, parents, and teachers. Through the compact, parents accepted responsibility for sending their children to school, regularly checking work, and communicating with teachers. Current student test scores were written on the top of the compact so that parents could assess their child's progress.

EVIDENCE OF SUCCESS

How successful was this school? An average of 15 volunteers worked on campus each day giving assistance in classrooms, the library, or the parent involvement office. Monthly parent training events attracted between 60 and 200 parents.

Student test scores improved dramatically; in the 1994–95 school year, 31% of students scored at about the 50th percentile in math and 14% scored at that level in reading. In 1995–1996, 61% of students scored above the 50th percentile in math and 34% scored above the 50th percentile in reading.

Parent involvement activities were coordinated through the school's parent involvement office. The school also housed offices for migrant student recruiters.

CONCLUSION

Establishing viable home–school partnerships is a complex process. Like families, very few involvement programs are exactly the same. Involving all families in their children's education requires time, resources, energy, and creativity. Although the task of establishing viable partnerships may seem overwhelming, practitioners may rest assured that there is no more important task. The impact of successful home, school, and community partnerships will have significant and lasting effects on the academic future of students.

APPLICATION
Working with Families

All schools face barriers to family involvement. However, some schools are more successful than others in using creative approaches to overcome these barriers and establish viable home–school partnerships. More successful schools have developed long-range plans aligned with school goals, re-structured schedules, reallocated teacher time, and tapped into community resources.

Schools with successful family involvement programs may be located in communities that are rural, inner city, urban, or small town. They may have large or small faculties. They may have the support of many businesses in the community or none at all. What they share in common is strong leadership and school staff who are willing to put forth extraordinary efforts to involve families in their children's education.

The principal's leadership is critical to the success of a family involvement plan. A principal who is committed to family involvement can guide faculty and staff in looking beyond the barriers to achieve solid home–school partnerships. However, the principal cannot implement a family involvement plan alone. Faculty and staff must believe in the purpose of the plan and be open-minded and nonjudgmental when considering opportunities for involving family members.

Open communication is a critical factor in developing effective home–school partnerships. In many communities, communication between home and school is hindered by differences in language, education, and socio-economic level, and culture. Teachers must understand and appreciate these differences and be able to communicate with all families regardless of their differences. Schools that have more successful family involvement usually have a highly visible, well-publicized point of contact for families. The point of contact might be the director of a parent resource center or a community member who serves as a family liaison. The point of contact can encourage families to visit the school either to volunteer, meet with the teachers, or simply to observe classes. The point of contact can also help to arrange communication with families that lack telephones or access to transportation.

Schools often must restructure to facilitate home–school partnerships. Parents who work evening hours or night shifts or have younger children may not be able to come to the school for activities. The principal and teachers may want to make home visits to ensure that all parents have opportunities to learn about the school.

Lack of time is a major barrier for teachers as well as parents. Some schools install telephones in classrooms and provide release time for teachers to enable them to call parents during the day. Substitute teachers may be brought in to allow teachers to make home visits during the instructional day. Some schools set up evening adult education programs with child care to encourage families to feel comfortable about coming to the school.

As school personnel became more aware of the problems and challenges that families face, they are able to find solutions to the barriers that prevent them from participating fully in school programs. The case study that follows focuses on one school's attempt to establish a school family involvement program. The principal, who plays a key role in getting the group together, encounters a number of barriers including parents who lack the confidence to participate and a teacher with a negative attitude. The characters in this case are fictitious, but the situation is not uncommon. As a teacher or principal, you are likely to encounter a similar situation.

CASE STUDY: *Developing a Plan*

Mrs. Rodriguez looked at the invitation from Elmhurst Elementary School with mixed feelings. She wanted to be like the other neighborhood mothers who helped with school events, but the thought of walking into a school again after so many years tied her stomach into knots. School had been a disconnected, miserable experience for her. She and her brothers and sisters worked in the fields with her parents and uncles harvesting apple crops. As the crops ripened from South to North, her family followed the other migrant families from one camp to the next. As a small child, she had loved her crisp yellow notebook, the Dick and Jane stories, and her red zippered pencil case. But as she moved into the upper elementary grades, the lessons got harder and keeping up became a struggle. Just when she was getting the hang of things, it was time for the family to move on. She never got to finish the stories in the reader or complete any math units. When she turned 15, she dropped out of school and worked in the fields full time. She wondered if anyone at any of the schools she had attended noticed that she was gone.

Now that she had children of her own, she wanted to be like the other parents; but the thought of going back to school made her cringe. She would have thrown the school invitation into the garbage if the principal hadn't come by the house to deliver the invitation personally. Mr. Jackson had seemed so friendly and reassuring. He really listened to her and asked for her opinions about what the school could do to make all parents feel welcome.

On the day of the meeting, Mrs. Tompkins, one of her neighbors who worked part time as the coordinator of the parent resource center, called and offered to come by and pick her up. Mrs. Rodriguez gladly accepted the offer because the bus ride to the school would have been long and tiring. Mrs. Tompkins stopped to pick up two other mothers along the way.

When the women arrived at the school, they joined six other parents and three teachers in the meeting room of the parent resource center. The school secretary brought in a fresh pot of coffee and cookies for the group. As the group chatted and filled their coffee cups, they talked about the upcoming state tests and the pressure it was placing on their children. Mr. Jackson was called to the telephone and listened as the manager of the local 7-11 store expressed his regrets about having to miss the meeting. Several minutes later the minister from the Baptist church on Main Street called to say he had a family emergency and wouldn't be able to join the group.

Mr. Jackson began the meeting by thanking everyone for coming. He explained that the purpose of the meeting was to develop a family involvement plan for the school. He described a series of staff development workshops that he had attended at the district office and smiled broadly as he expressed his enthusiasm for carrying out the new ideas he had heard. Miss Vaupel, who had been a teacher in the school for more than 20 years, commented wryly that she had heard it all before. Ignoring her comment, Mr. Jackson said he wanted the group to serve as an Action Team. Their first task would be to conduct a needs assessment of the community to identify what was working for the school, who was involved, what teachers expect of parents, and what parents expect of teachers. Miss Vaupel leaned forward in her chair and said in an authoritative voice, "We did this 10 years ago and nothing came of it. Most of the parents in the neighborhoods surrounding the school are too busy to get involved. Why bother?"

The other two teachers, on the team, relatively new to the school and the teaching profession, looked surprised by Miss Vaupel's comments. They exchanged glances with each other, sat quietly, and avoided making eye contact with the other members of the group.

Mr. Jackson talked animatedly about his vision and what he hoped to accomplish with more families involved in the school. He directed questions at the parents soliciting their input and tried to stimulate discussion. Before others could respond, Miss Vaupel interrupted with more negative comments. Mr. Jackson made numerous attempts to encourage the group to participate. He tried to counter Miss Vaupel's comments by redirecting her negative remarks. He was intense in discussing his ideas for a school family involvement plan, and continued to probe for ideas and suggestions from the group.

The two new teachers said they weren't familiar with the neighborhoods or families and preferred not to comment. As the principal talked about his ideas, the two new teachers crossed and uncrossed their legs and shifted their weight in their chairs. Miss Vaupel frequently glanced down at some papers on her lap that were labeled "State Competency Tests." The mothers listened politely to the principal, but hesitated to speak.

The parent coordinator tried to inject some ideas into the conversation, but stopped when she saw that the teachers and parents weren't saying anything. Perhaps, she thought, it would be more efficient if Mr. Jackson drew up the plans and presented them at the next meeting of the group.

CASE STUDY DISCUSSION GUIDE

Themes: Developing a school family involvement plan; strategies for getting input from parents; barriers to leadership.

Actors

A. How would you characterize Mrs. Rodriguez, Mrs. Tompkins, Mr. Jackson, and Miss Vaupel? (List each person's name, leaving space to list one-, two-, or three-word descriptors for each actor.)

Probes

1. How do you think each of the actors in this case felt before the committee meeting? After the meeting?
2. How does Mrs. Rodriguez view her role as a parent?
3. How does Mrs. Tompkins view her role as parent coordinator?
4. What kind of principal is Mr. Jackson?

Issues

B. What are the major issues in this case?

Probes

1. What actions on the part of the principal and the parent coordinator encouraged Mrs. Rodriguez to attend the meeting?
2. Was the membership of the Action Team well thought out? Who was missing?
3. Why do you think Miss Vaupel behaved the way she did?
4. Why do you think the principal had such a difficult time getting the members of the group to participate?
5. Why didn't the new teachers offer any opinions?
6. Why didn't the parents offer any opinions?

Problems or Conflicts

What are the problems or conflicts in this case? Make a list of these problems or conflicts and specify whether you think they stem from personal or institutional origins. Now, examine the list further. Can you separate the items on your list into primary and secondary subcategories? (After completing this last step, you may find it easier to suggest solutions to the problems or conflicts in this case.)

Solutions

A. Do you think the principal did his homework to prepare for the meeting?
   1. If yes, what action did he take?
   2. If no, what do you think he failed to do?
B. What can be done to develop a comprehensive family involvement plan at this school?

Probes

1. What could Mr. Jackson do to encourage the Action Team to return for another meeting?
2. How can the parent coordinator help the principal lead the Action Team?
3. How can more community members be involved in developing the school plan?

SUPPLEMENTAL ACTIVITIES

FIELD EXPERIENCE A

School-Based Activity

As you observe and participate in schools, look for opportunities to discover how schools involve families in school activities. Interview the principal to find out what, if anything, has been done to establish a family involvement program at the school. What barriers to family involvement are there at this particular school? What is the nature and level of parent participation?

Interview three different teachers to discover how they view parent involvement. Have they participated in any efforts to establish action teams or family involvement programs? What staff development would help them interact with parents?

FIELD EXPERIENCE B

Community-Based Activity

Research local media (newspapers, television, and radio) for evidence of school-community partnerships. What is the nature and scope of these partnerships? As a result of your research, are you able to identify community leaders who support school programs?

RESPONSE JOURNAL PROMPTS

As an alternative to using the **Case Study Discussion Guide,** facilitators may ask participants to reflect on the case and construct a written response to the following prompts:

1. What could Mr. Jackson have done to include community business members in the meeting?

2. How could Mr. Jackson have handled Miss Vaupel's negativity?

3. How could Mr. Jackson have helped the parent coordinator and teachers take stronger leadership roles?

4. How would you go about setting up a family involvement program at a school? Include the essential steps you would take.

ROLE PLAYING AND REFLECTION EXERCISE

To better understand how difficult it is to establish communication between school personnel and families, participate in a role play meeting that Mr. Jackson held. Assume the role of one of the three teachers, the parents, the principal, or the parent coordinator. Following the role play, discuss the different positions each person took. What do these positions teach you about establishing action teams?

DISCUSSION
Brainstorm practical ways to implement a family involvement program including conducting a needs assessment, finding resources, disseminating information, keeping everyone's motivation high, and achieving short-term and long-range goals.

IMPLICATIONS FOR FAMILY INVOLVEMENT
Construct a list of ways family members can provide leadership to establish and maintain a viable action team at their child's school. Share your lists with the group.

REFERENCES

Batey, C. S. (1996). *Parents are lifesavers: A handbook for parent involvement in schools.* Thousand Oaks, CA: Corwin Press.

Canter, L., & Canter, M. (1991). *Parents on your side.* Santa Monica, CA: Lee Canter & Associates.

Epstein, J. L., Coates, L., Salinas, K. C., Sanders, M. G., & Simon, B. S. (1997). *School, family, and community partnerships: Your handbook for action.* Thousand Oaks, CA: Corwin Press.

Hanhan, S. F. (1998). Parent-teacher communication: Who's talking? In M. L. Fuller & G. Olsen (Eds.), *Home-school relations: Working successfully with parents and families.* Boston: Allyn & Bacon.

Laboratory for Student Success. (1997a). Positive communication between parents and teachers. In *Partnerships: A guide for parents* (No. 100). Philadelphia: Laboratory for Student Success.

Laboratory for Student Success. (1997b). Ideas for positive communication between parents and teachers. In *Partnerships: A guide for teachers* (No. 103). Philadelphia: Laboratory for Student Success.

SERVE (n.d.) *Understanding comprehensive reform: An in-depth look at nine essential components* (Component Six, report no. ED-01-CO-0015). U.S. Department of Education, Office of Educational Research and Improvement. Retrieved from http://www.serve.org/UCR/UCRCompSixpage2.html

STAR Center, (2000a). *Creating family friendly schools: A guidebook for trainers.* Denver, CO: RMC Research Corporation.

STAR Center. (2000b). *Creating family friendly schools: A guidebook for trainers* (Module 5, Handout 2, p. 1). Denver, CO: RMC Research Corporation.

Appendix A

BIBLIOGRAPHY AND RESOURCES

CLASSROOM RESEARCH

Bogdan, R. C., & Biklen, S. K. (1998). *Qualitative research for education: An introduction to theory and methods* (3rd ed.). Boston: Allyn & Bacon.

Borich, G. D. (1999). *Observation skills for effective teaching* (3rd ed.). Upper Saddle River, NJ: Merrill/Prentice Hall.

Noffke, S. E., & Stevenson, R. B. (Eds.). (1995). *Educational action research: Becoming practically critical.* New York: Teachers College Press.

Seidman, I. (1998). *Interviewing as qualitative research: A guide for researchers in education and the social sciences* (2nd ed.). New York: Teachers College Press.

EARLY FIELD EXPERIENCES

McIntyre, D. J., & Byrd, D. M. (1996). Preparing tomorrow's teachers: The field experience. *Teacher Education Yearbook IV, Association of Teacher Educators.* Thousand Oaks, CA: Corwin Press.

Slick, G. A. (Ed.). (1995). *The field experience: Creating successful programs for new teachers.* Thousand Oaks, CA: Corwin Press.

Slick, G. A. (Ed.). (1995). *Making the difference for teachers: The field experience in actual practice.* Thousand Oaks, CA: Corwin Press.

Slick, G. A. (Ed.). (1995). *Preparing new teachers: Operating successful field experience programs.* Thousand Oaks, CA: Corwin Press.

Wiseman, D. L., Cooner, D. D., & Knight, S. L. (1999). *Becoming a teacher in a field-based setting: An introduction to education and classrooms.* Belmont, CA: Wadsworth.

GENERAL RESOURCES FOR FAMILY MEMBERS

AEL. (2003). *Family Connections K–1*. Lanham, MD: ScarecrowEducation. (Also available in Spanish.) *http://www.ael.org*

Carnegie Foundation. (1999). *Great transitions: Preparing adolescents for a new century* (chap. 3). New York: Author. Retrieved July 1, 1999, from *http://www.carnegie.org/sub/pubs/reports/great_transitions/grchpt3html*

Koralek, D. (n.d.). *Ready*set*read for families*. Washington, DC: Corporation for National Service, U.S. Department of Education, and U.S. Department of Health and Human Services.

Macfarlane, E. C. (1994). *Children's literacy development: Suggestions for parent involvement*. Bloomington, IN: ERIC Clearinghouse on Reading, English, and Communication. (ERIC Document Reproduction Service No. ED365979)

Nathenson-Mejia, S. (1994). Bridges between home and school: Literacy-building activities for non-native English speaking homes. *The Journal of Educational Issues of Language Minority Students, 14,* 149–164. Available from *http://www.ncela.gwu.edu/miscpubs/jeilms/vol14/nathenso.htm*

North Central Regional Educational Laboratory. (1999). *What is my kid thinking? Understanding how your middle schooler learns*. Available from *http://www.ncrel.org/Tech&Education2.html*

Schwartz, W. (1999). *How to recognize and develop your children's special talents* (ERIC Digest No. 122). New York: ERIC Clearinghouse on Urban Education.

Schwartz, W. (1999, July). *Family math for urban students and parents* (ERIC Digest No. 146). New York: ERIC Clearinghouse on Urban Education. (ERIC Document Reproduction Service No. ED432630)

U.S. Department of Education, Office of Educational Research and Improvement. (1999). *Helping your child learn math*. Washington, DC: Author. Available from *http://www.ed.gov/pubs/parents/Math/index.html*

Venezky, R. L. (1995). *The read* write *now! partners tutoring program*. Washington, DC: U.S. Department of Education.

WEB SITES

Children's Defense Fund
http://www.childrensdefense.org/

COMPASS Resource: Parents and Teachers
http://www.compassinc.com/resources.html

Cybergrrl Safety Net—Domestic Violence Resources
http://www.cybergrrl.com/dv.html

ERIC Clearinghouse on Elementary and Early Childhood Education
http://www.ericeece.org

National Clearinghouse on Child Abuse and Neglect Information
http://www.calib.com/nccanch

National Clearinghouse on Families and Youth
http://www.ncfy.com

National Middle School Association
http://www.nmsa.org

National Parent Information Network (NPIN)
http://www.npin.org

CULTURE, POVERTY, AND ETHNICITY

Burnette, J. (1999, November). *Critical behaviors and strategies for teaching culturally diverse students* (ERIC/OSEP Digest No. E584). Reston, VA: ERIC Clearinghouse on Disabilities and Gifted Education. (ERIC Document Reproduction Service No. ED435147)

Catalano, R. F., Lober, R., & McKinney, K. C. (1999). School and community interventions to prevent serious and violent offending. *Juvenile Justice Bulletin,* 1–12.

Gibbs, J. T., Huange, L. N., & Associates. (1989). *Children of color.* San Francisco: Jossey-Bass.

Hightower, A. M., Nathanson, S. P., & Wimberly, G. L. (1997). *Meeting the educational needs of homeless children and youth: A resource for schools and communities.* Washington, DC: U.S. Department of Education, Office of Elementary and Secondary Education.

Kendall, F. E. (1996). *Diversity in the classroom: New approaches to the education of young children* (2nd ed.). Williston, VT: Teachers College Press.

King, J. E., Hollins, E. R., & Hayman, W. C. (Eds). (1997). *Preparing teachers for cultural diversity.* New York: Teachers College Press.

Moles, O. C. (Ed.). (1996). *Reaching all families: Creating family-friendly schools.* Washington, DC: U.S. Department of Education, Office of Educational Research and Improvement. Retrieved October 7, 1999, from *http://www.ed.gov/pubs/ReachFam*

Ryskamp, G., & Ryskamp, P. (1996). *A student's guide to Mexican American genealogy.* Phoenix, AZ: Oryx Press.

Santos, R., Fowler, S., Corso, R., & Burns, D. (2000). Acceptance, acknowledgment, and adaptability: Selecting culturally and linguistically appropriate early childhood materials. *Teaching Exceptional Children, 32*(3), 14–22.

WEB SITES

African American resources
http://www.blackguest.com/link.htm

Asian American resources
http://www.ai.mit.edu/people/irie/aar

Azteca Web Page (for Mexicans, Chicanos, and Mexican Americans)
http://www.mexica.net

Complexities of communicating with Asian and Pacific Islander children and their families
http://eric-web.tc.columbia.edu/digests/dig94.html

Institute for Children and Poverty
http://www.homesforthehomeless.com/abouticpframe.html

National Association for the Education of Homeless Children and Youth
www.naehcy.org

National Center for Children in Poverty
http://www.nccp.org/

National Center for Homeless Education
www.serve.org/nche

National Center for Research on Cultural Diversity and Second Language Learning
http://zzyx.ucsc.edu/cntr/cntr.html

National Law Center on Homelessness & Poverty
www.nlchp.org

Resources for Native American Families
http://www.familyvillage.wisc.edu/frc_natv.htm

Written in Spanish, a variety of resources for parents to promote family involvement
http://www.pta.org/parentinvolvement/spanish/index.asp.

GAY MALE AND LESBIAN FAMILIES

McFarland, W., & Dupuis, M. (2001). The legal duty to protect gay and lesbian students from violence in school. *Professional School Counseling, 4*(3), 171–179.

Patterson, C. J. (1995). Families of the lesbian baby boom: Parents' division of labor and children's adjustment. *Developmental Psychology, 31,* 115–123.

Remafedi, G. (1999). Sexual orientation and youth suicide. *Journal of the American Medical Association, 282*(13), 1291–1292.

Ryan, M. (2003). *Ask the teacher: A practitioner's guide to teaching and learning in the diverse classroom.* Boston: Allyn & Bacon.

Savin-Williams, R. (1994). The disclosure to families of same-sex attractions by lesbian, gay, and bisexual youths. *Journal of Research on Adolescence, 3,* 49–68.

Tasker, F. L., & Goloombok, S. (1997). *Growing up in a lesbian family: Effects on child development.* New York: Guilford Press.

WEB SITES

Diversity resources
http://www.inform.umd.edu/EdRes/Topic/Diversity/

Pathways to Diversity on the World Wide Web
http://www.lanl.gov/orgs/dvo/DvoLibrary/Index.html

FAMILIES WITH CHILDREN WHO HAVE SPECIAL NEEDS

Alper, S., Schloss, P. J., & Schloss, C. N. (1996). Families of children with disabilities in elementary and middle school: Advocacy models and strategies. *Exceptional Children, 62,* 261–270.

Bryan, T., & Sullivan-Burstein, K. (1997). Homework how-to's. *Teaching Exceptional Children, 29*(6), 32–37.

Burnette, J. (1998, March). *Reducing the disproportionate representation of minority students in special education* (ERIC/OSEP Digest No. E566). Reston, VA: ERIC Clearinghouse on Disabilities and Gifted Education. (ERIC Document Reproduction Service No. ED417501)

Epstein, M., Munk, D., Bursuck, W., Polloway, E., & Jayanthi, M. (1999). Strategies for improving home-school communication about homework for students with disabilities. *The Journal of Special Education, 33*(3), 166–176.

Meyers, D. J., & Vadasy, P. F. (1994). *Sibshops: Workshops for siblings of children with special needs.* Baltimore: Brookes.

Powell, T. H., & Gallagher, P. A. (1993). *Brothers, & sisters: A special part of exceptional families* (2nd ed.). Baltimore: Brookes.

Turnbull, A. P., & Turnbull, H. R. (1997). *Families, professionals, and exceptionality: A special partnership* (3rd ed.). Upper Saddle River, NJ: Merrill/Prentice Hall.

Turnbull, A. P., & Turnbull, H. R. (2000). Fostering family-professional partnerships. In M. E. Snell & F. Brown (Eds.), *Instruction of students with severe disabilities.* Upper Saddle River, NJ: Merrill/Prentice Hall.

WEB SITES

Children's Defense Fund
http://www.childrensdefense.org/

Council for Exceptional Children
http://www.cec.sped.org?

Disability resources
http://www.icdi.wvu.edu/Others.htm

Family Village
http://familyvillage.wisc.edu/

SCHOOL, FAMILY, COMMUNITY, AND BUSINESS PARTNERSHIPS

The following resources serve as guides to establishing and maintaining effective family involvement programs or home, school, and community partnerships.

Batey, C. S. (1996). *Parents are lifesavers: A handbook for parent involvement in schools.* Thousand Oaks, CA: Corwin Press.

Catalano, R. F., Loeber, R., & McKinney, K. C. (1999). School and community interventions to prevent serious and violent offending. *Juvenile Justice Bulletin,* 1–12.

Community Partnerships. (1998). Education Week on the Web. Retrieved October 26, 1999, from *http://www.edweek.org/context/topics/communita.htm*

Danzberger, J., Bodinger-deUriarte, C., & Clark, M. (1996). *A guide to promising practices in educational partnerships.* Washington, DC: U.S. Department of Education, Office of Educational Research and Improvement. Retrieved October 26, 1999, from *http://www.ed.gov/pubs/PromPact/prom1.html*

Davis, D. (1998, June 9). *Partnerships for student success.* Baltimore Center on Families, Communities, Schools and Children's Learning. Retrieved October 26, 1999, from *http://www.cyfc.umn.edu/Learn/partnerships.html*

Epstein, J. L., Coates, L., Jansorn, N. R., Salinas, K. C., Sanders, M. G., Simon, B. S., et al. (2002). *School, family, and community partnerships: Your handbook for action* (2nd ed.). Thousand Oaks, CA: Corwin Press.

Fuller, M. L., & Olsen, G. (1998). *Home-school relations: Working successfully with parents and families.* Boston: Allyn, & Bacon.

Lewis, A. (1997). *Building bridges: Eight case studies of schools and communities working together.* Chicago: Cross City Campaign for Urban School Reform.

CHILDREN AND ADOLESCENT LITERATURE FEATURING VARIOUS FAMILY STRUCTURES

GENERAL FAMILY

All Families Are Different by Sol Gordon
All Kinds of Families by Norma Simon
Amelia Bedelia's Family Album by Peggy Parish
Beginnings: How Families Come to Be by Virginia Kroll
Big Sister, Little Sister by Marci Curtis
Brothers and Sisters by Ellen Senisi
Celebrating Families by Rosmarie Hausherr
Daddy Will Be There by Lois G. Grambling
Families by Ann Morris
Families by Meredith Tax
Families Are Different by Nina Pellegrini
Families Are Funny by Nan Hunt
Family For Sale by Eth Clifford
Family Tree by Pierre Coran
Grandfather's Journey by Allen Say

In Daddy's Arms I Am Tall by Javaka Steptoe, and Others
Is Your Family Like Mine? by Lois Abramchik
The Keeping Quilt by Patricia Polacco
The Patchwork Quilt by Valerie Flournoy
Love to Mama: A Tribute to Mothers by Pat Mora, and Others
Love You Forever by Robert N. Munsch
Me and My Family Tree by Joan Sweeney
Me, & You: A Mother-Daughter Album by Lisa Theising
My Family Tree: A Bird's Eye View by Nina Laden
My Great-Aunt Arizona by Gloria Houston
One Hundred Is a Family by Pam Munoz Ryan
The Relatives Came by Cynthia Rylant
Sister For Sale by Michelle M. Adams
Who's in a Family? by Robert Skutch
Who's Who in My Family? by Loreen Leedy

ADOPTION

A Family for Jamie: An Adoption Story by Suzanne Bloom
A Forever Family by Roslyn Banish
A Koala for Katie: An Adoption Story by Jonathan London
A Mother for Choco by Keiko Kasza
Abby by Jeannette F. Caines
Adoption Is For Always by Linda W. Girard
Beginnings: How Families Come to Be by Virginia Kroll
Benjamin Bear Gets a New Family by Deborah Joy
The Chosen Baby by Valentina P. Wassen
The Day We Met You by Phoebe Koehler
Did My First Mother Love Me? by Katherine Miller
Goose by Molly Bang
Happy Adoption Day! by John McCutcheon
Heaven by Angela Johnson
How I Was Adopted: Samantha's Story by Joanna Cole
How It Feels to Be Adopted by Jill Krementz
Let's Talk about It: Adoption by Fred Rogers
My Real Family by Emily A. McCully
Pablo's Tree by Pat Mora
Pinky and Rex and the New Baby by James Howe
Real Sisters by Susan Wright
Tell Me Again About the Night I Was Born by Jamie Lee Curtis
This Is How We Became a Family: An Adoption Story by Wayne Willis
Transracial Adoption: Children and Parents Speak by Constance Pohl, and Kathy Harris
Twice-Upon-A-Time: Born and Adopted by Eleanora Patterson
Two Birthdays for Beth by Gay Cronin
When Joel Comes Home by Susi Gregg Fowler
William Is My Brother by Jane T. Schnitter

Zachary's New Home: A Story for Foster and Adopted Children by Geraldine M. and Paul B. Blomquest
Zoe & Columbo by Susan Shreve

INTERNATIONAL ADOPTION

Allison by Allen Say
An Mei's Strange and Wondrous Journey by Stephan Molnar-Fenton
The Best Single Mom in the World: How I Was Adopted by Mary Zisk
Carolyn's Story by Perry Schwartz
Chinese Eyes by Marjorie Ann Waybill
Families Are Different by Nina Pellegrini
Heart of Mine: A Story of Adoption by Dan, and Lotta Hojer
I Love You Like Crazy Cakes by Rose A. Lewis
Jin Woo by Eve Bunting
Katie-Bo: An Adoption Story by Iris L. Fisher
Lucy's Family Tree by Karen H. Schreck
Mommy Far, Mommy Near: An Adoption Story by Carol A. Peacock
Over the Moon: An Adoption Tale by Karen Katz
Through Moon and Stars and Night Skies by Ann Warren Turner
We Adopted You, Benjamin Koo by Linda Wolvoord Girard
When You Were Born in China by Sara Dorrow
When You Were Born in Korea by Brian Boyd

BLENDED AND STEP FAMILIES

All Families Are Different by Sol Gordon
Amber Brown Wants Extra Credit by Paula Danziger
Eliza's Daddy by Janthe Thomas
Everett Anderson's 1-2-3 by Lucille Clifton
Getting Used to Harry by Cari Best
How Do I Feel about My Stepfamily by Julie Johnson
Let's Talk About Living in a Blended Family by Elizabeth Weitzman
Like Jake and Me by Mavis Jukes
My Mother's Getting Married by Joan Drescher
My Parents Are Divorced, Too: A Book for Kids by Kids by Melanie, Annie, and Stephen Ford, as told to Jan Blackstone-Ford and Steven Ford
My Real Family: A Child's Book About Living in a Stepfamily by Doris E. Sanford
My Wicked Stepmother by Leach Norman
Robert Lives with His Grandparents by Martha W. Hickman
Room for a Stepdaddy by Jean Thor Cook
Sam Is My Half-Brother by Lizi Boyd
Sarah, Plain and Tall by Patricia MacLachlan
She's Not My Real Mother by Judith Vigna
Skylark by Patricia MacLachlan
Totally Uncool by Janice Levy
We're Growing Together by Candice F. Ransom
What I'll Remember When I'm a Grownup by Gina Wilner-Pardo

When I Am a Sister by Robin Ballard
When We Married Gary by Anna G. Hines

DEATH OF A FAMILY MEMBER

A Heartbreaking Work of Staggering Genius by Dave Eggers
After Charlotte's Mom Died by Cornelia Spelman
BFG by Roald Dahl
Family Tree by Katherine Ayres
Geranium Morning: A Book about Grief by E. Sandy Powell
I Miss You by Pat Thomas
James and the Giant Peach by Roald Dahl
Out of the Dust by Karen Hesse
Plum and Jaggers by Susan R. Shreve
Walk Two Moons by Sharon Creech

DIVORCE

Always, Always by Crescent Dragonwagon
At Daddy's on Saturday by Linda W. Girard
Charlie Anderson by Barbara Abererombie
Confessions of a Divorced Kid by Steve Sullivan
Daddy by Jeannette F. Caines
Daddy Day, Daughter Day by Larry King
Dear Daddy by John Schindel
Dear Mr. Henshaw by Beverly Cleary
Dinosaur's Divorce: A Guide for Changing Families by L. K. Brown
Good-bye, Daddy by Brigitte Weninger
Gracie by Robin Ballard
Grandma Without Me by Judith Vigna
I Don't Want to Talk About It by Jeanie F. Ransom
I Have Two Families by Doris W. Helmering
I Live with Daddy by Judith Vigna
I Think Divorce Stinks by Marcia L. Lebowitz
It's Not Your Fault KoKo Bear by Vicky Lansky
Let's Talk About It: Divorce by Fred Rogers
Let's Talk About Your Parent's Divorce by Elizabeth Weitzman
Loon Summer by Barbara Santucci
Mama and Paddy Bear's Divorce by Cornelia Spelman
Megan's Two Houses: A Story of Adjustment by Erica Jong
Mommy and Daddy Are Divorced by Patricia Perry
My Mother Got Married by Barbara Park
My Mother's House, My Father's House by C. B. Christiansen
My Mother Is Not Married to My Father by Jean Davies Okimoto
On the Day His Daddy Left by Eric J. Adams
On With the Show! Featuring Brenda Dubrowski by Barbara Aiello
Priscilla Twice by Judith Caseley
Since Dad Left by Caroline Binch

Two Homes by Claire Masurel
Two Homes to Live In: A Child's View of Divorce by Barbara Hazen
Two Places to Sleep by Joan Schuchaman
The Un-Wedding by Babette Cole
Where Has Daddy Gone? by Tnady Osman
Why Are We Getting a Divorce? by Peter Mayle

FOSTER FAMILIES

A Mother for Choco by Keiko Kasza
Dancing Shoes by Noel Streatfeild
For Your Own Good: A Child's Book About Foster Care by Doris Sanford
Heidi by Johanna Spyri
I Miss My Foster Parents by Stefon Herbert
Jason's Story by Deborah Anderson
Let's Talk About Foster Homes by Elizabeth Weitzman
Madeline by Ludwig Bemelmans
Mama One, Mama Two by Patricia MacLachlan
The Secret Garden by Frances Hodgson Burnett
Zachary's New Home: A Story for Foster and Adopted Children by Geraldine M. Blomquest

GRANDPARENTS AND ELDERS

A Special Trade by Sally Wittnian
A Visit to Grandma's by Nancy Carlson
Always Grandma by Vaunda M. Nelson
Blow Me a Kiss, Miss Lilly by Nancy W. Carlstrom
By the Dawn's Early Light by Karen Ackerman
Gramma's Walk by Anna G. Hines
Grandma Drives a Motor Bed by Diane J. Hamm
Grandma's Hands by Dolores Johnson
Grandma's Wheelchair by Lorraine Henriod
Grandmother and I by Helen E. Buckley
Grandpa's Song by Tony Johnston
Granpa by John Burningham
Great-Uncle Alfred Forgets by Ben Shecter
How Does It Feel to Be Old? by Norma Farber
I Dance in My Red Pajamas by Edith T. Hurd
Kevin's Grandma by Barbara Williams
Loop the Loop by Barbara Dugan
Luka's Quilt by Georgia Guback
Mandy's Grandmother by Liesel M. Skorpen
My Grandma Has Black Hair by Mary Hoffman
My Great-Grandpa Joe by Marilyn Gelfand
Nana Upstairs and Nana Downstairs by Tomie dePaola
Now One Foot, Now the Other by Tomie dePaola
Robert Lives with His Grandparents by Martha W. Hickman

Sachiho Means Happiness by Salai Kirniho
Singing with Momma Lou by Linda J. Altman
Sunshine Home by Eve Bunting
Through Grandpa's Eyes by Patricia MacLachlin
Tutu Kane and Grandpa by Nancy A. Mower
Two Mrs. Gibsons by Toyomi Igus
The Two of Them by Aliki
The Wednesday Surprise by Eve Bunting
When I Am Old With You by Angela Johnson

HOMELESS FAMILIES

A Ceiling of Stars by Ann Howard Creel
A Chair for My Mother by Vera B. Williams
A Chance to Grow by E. Sandy Powell
Being Poor by Janet Rosenberg
Bye, Bye, Bali Kai by Harriet M. Luger
Changing Places: A Kid's View of Shelter Living by Margie Chalofsky
Cooper's Tale by Ralph da Costa Nunez
December by Eve Bunting
Elsa, Star of the Shelter! by Jacqueline Wilson
Erik Is Homeless by Keith Elliot Greenberg
Fly Away Home by Eve Bunting
Gracie's Girl by Ellen Wittlinger
Home Is Where We Live: Life in a Shelter Through a Young Girl's Eyes by Kimiko
Homeless by Bernard Wolf
The Leaves in October by Karen Ackerman
Lives Turned Upside Down by Jim Hubbard
Mandy's House: The Story of a Homeless Family Who Finds a New Place to Live by Ruth Spangler
Motley the Cat by Mary Fedden
No Place to Be: Voices of Homeless Children by Judith Berek
Our Wish by Ralph da Costa Nunez
Tight Times by Barbara Hazen (in Spanish: *Tiempos Duros*)
Way Home by Elizabeth Hathorn

SAME-GENDER PARENTS

123: A Family Counting Book by Bobbie Combs
ABC: A Family Alphabet Book by Bobbie Combs
Amy Asks a Question . . . : Grandma—What's a Lesbian? by Jeanne Arnold
Anna Day and the 0-Ring by Elaine Wickens
Asha's Mums by Rosamund Elwin
Belinda's Bouquet by Leslea Newman
Best Best Colors by Eric Hoffman (in Spanish: *Los Mejores Colores*)
The Daddy Machine by Johnny Valentine
Daddy's Roommate by Michael Willhoite
Daddy's Wedding by Michael Willhoite

The Duke Who Outlawed Jelly Beans by Johnny Valentine

Elliott & Win by Carolyn Meyer

Families by Meredith Tax

Gloria Goes to Gay Pride by Leslea Newman

Heather Has Two Mommies by Leslea Newman

How Would You Feel If Your Dad Was Gay? by Ann Heron

Is Your Family Like Mine? by Lois Abramchik

Jennifer Has Two Daddies by Priscilla Galloway

Jenny Lives with Eric and Martin by Susanne Bosche, translated by Louis Mackay

Lots of Mommies by Janc Severance

Lucy Goes to the Country by Joe Kennedy

Mama Eat Ant, Yuck! by Barbara Lynn Edmonds

My Two Uncles by Judith Vigna

One Dad, Two Dads, Brown Dad, Blue Dads by Johnny Valentine

Saturday Is Pattyday by Leslea Newman

Taking Sides by Norma Klein

The Generous Jefferson Bartleby Jones by Forman Brown

Two Moms, the Zark, and Me by Johnny Valentine

When Grown-Ups Fall in Love by Barbara Lynn Edmonds

When Megan Went Away by Jane Severance

Your Family, My Family by Joan Drescher

Zach's Story: Growing Up with Same-Sex Parents by Keith Elliot Greenberg

SINGLE-PARENT FAMILIES

The Best Single Mom in the World: How I Was Adopted by Mary Zisk

By the Dawn's Early Light by Karen Ackerman

Dear Mr. Henshaw by Beverly Cleary

Do I Have a Daddy? A Story About a Single-Parent Child by Jeanne Warren Lindsay

Everett Anderson's Christmas by Lucille Clifton

Gettin' Through Thursday by Melrose Cooper

Goodnight, Daddy by Angela Seward

I Love My Mother by Paul Zindel

Junebug by Alice Mead

Let's Talk About Living With a Single Parent by Elizabeth Weitzman

Let's Talk About Living With Your Single Dad by Melanie Ann Apel

Ma Dear's Aprons by Pat McKissack

Mom Is Single by Lena Paris

Mommy and Me by Ourselves Again by Judith Vigna

The Moonlight Man by Betty R. Wright

My Kind of Family: A Book for Kids in Single-Parent Homes by Michele Lash

Soldier Mom by Alice Mend

Totally Uncool by Janice Levy

When Mama Comes Home Tonight by Eileen Spinelli

List provided by Karl Bell and Deanna Gilmore (2002) Unpublished Paper.

Appendix B

SUGGESTED PROCEDURES FOR TEACHING AND LEARNING FROM CASE STUDIES

This appendix contains descriptions of two different sets of procedures for learning from case studies. The first set is directed to those who may be given an assignment to read the case and to analyze it independently. The second set of procedures will be helpful to those who will be leading a discussion of the case in a group setting.

INDEPENDENT ANALYSIS OF CASES

The following step-by-step suggestions for case analysis are taken from the book *Case Studies for Teacher Problem Solving*, by Silverman, Welty, & Lyon (1992).*

1. **Understand the assignment in context.** Your instructor will probably assign one case at a time along with some study questions or issues to direct your thinking. Each case will most likely be accompanied or preceded by traditional textbook assignments. These may alert you to theoretical concepts related to the case. Therefore, before you begin to read the case, be sure that you understand the overall framework within which the case is being used and the points your instructor may want to emphasize.

2. **Read the case for an overview.** Try reading the case first rather quickly, to get a general idea of what it is about: What happened, who the main characters are, what the problems are, and how the issues in the case relate to the overall assignment.

---

*Reprinted with permission of the publisher from Silverman, R., Welty, W. M., & Lyon, S. (1992). *Case Studies for Teacher Problem Solving*. New York: McGraw-Hill.

3. **Analyze the case.** Read the case again, this time more carefully. Try to make sense of the study questions assigned by your instructor. Make notes of main characters and their relationships with each other. Try to understand the problems, both obvious and hidden. Try to understand the point of view of the case; that is, determine who is providing the information. Identify what impact this perspective may have on the information in the case. Make a list of questions you have about the content, and identify any other information you would like to have. At the end of this stage you should have constructed a list of problems and an understanding of the cause of these problems.

4. **Seek outside information.** You may want to turn to outside sources for help in understanding the problems you have identified and to develop solutions. Go to the textbook, especially the chapter assigned to accompany the case. Anything that helps you understand the case better at this point is fair game to use.

5. **Develop solutions.** Ultimately, cases call for solutions to problems; not to determine the one right answer, but to focus analysis and to prepare you for a real world of teacher decision making and action. Relate your solutions to your analysis of the problems. There are no perfect decisions, so think of both the strengths and weaknesses of your solutions. Every good solution has a downside; it may not negate your solution, but you should try at least to understand the negatives as well as the positives of your solutions. Prepare to argue for your position in class. Go to class with a relevant theory that supports your position. Be ready to take risks. The case class is a teaching laboratory, the case is a lab experiment, and you are the social scientist seeking to test your ideas.*

GROUP DISCUSSION OF CASES

The following procedures for teaching cases during a class or seminar format are taken from *Suggested Procedures for Conducting Case Study Discussions* (Diss & Thompson, 1994). Their work appears in *Instructional Cases for Preservice and Student Teachers: Case Studies for Teacher Training and Educational Leadership,* Diane Foucar-Szocki (Ed.), Harrisonburg, VA: Commonwealth Center for the Education of Teachers, James Madison, University, 1994, 26.

We encourage discussion leaders to review the following general procedures for teaching cases, and then to read the discussion guides written specifically for each case in order to organize a discussion plan suited to their particular circumstances (Diss & Thompson, 1994).

1. Distribute a copy of the case along with a Wait Sheet (see Attachment) to each participant. Tell the participants to read the case, then immediately write a brief reaction to it and at least one question they have about the case. Explain that the Wait Sheet also contains space for

---

*Silverman, R., Welty, W. M., & Lyon, S. (1992). *Case studies for teacher problem solving.* New York: McGraw-Hill.

them to jot down ideas as they surface during the discussion. By doing this, they won't forget to contribute these ideas later during the discussion.

2. Before beginning the actual discussion of the case, ask participants to share the questions they wrote on their Wait Sheet with each other in pairs or in small groups. The discussion leader should not comment on what students say at this point. The purpose of this step is to help participants become comfortable with the idea of sharing and responding.

3. Begin discussing the case with the whole group, using the probes listed under each of the four categories (Actors, Issues, Problems or Conflicts, and Solutions) from the discussion guide. We suggest that discussion leaders list the four categories on a board or flip chart at the beginning of the discussion. As the discussion unfolds, participants' comments can be written under each of these categories. Doing this will help participants keep track visually of the discussion as it proceeds.

4. Have participants wear nametags with their first names clearly visible and call on them by name. Doing this will allow you to move the discussion along at a smooth pace. (Caution: Remember that some cases won't necessarily lead to animated discussions. Participants may need to think carefully about the case and what they hear others saying; as a result, they may be hesitant to blurt out comments due to intense concentration. Provide sufficient "wait time.")

5. Near the end of the discussion, ask participants if they have any remaining ideas listed on their Wait Sheets that they would like to contribute to the discussion.

6. At the conclusion of the discussion, ask participants to summarize (either orally, in writing, or both) the key details and concepts of the case.

ATTACHMENT—WAIT SHEET

Upon completion of reading this case (and prior to group discussion), please write a brief response to the following:

1. My initial reaction to this case is: _____

_____

_____

_____

_____

_____

2. A question I have about this case is: _____

_____

_____

_____

_____

_____

As the group discusses the case, questions or ideas may come to you that you think are important to understanding the case. Use the space below or on the back to put these thoughts "on reserve" as a reminder to include them in the discussion.

Appendix C

GENERAL GUIDELINES FOR EARLY FIELD EXPERIENCES

Early field experiences provide rich opportunities for preservice teachers, and those in related career preparation programs, to visit schools and community-based social service agencies to learn about the dynamics of classroom instruction and the relationships among home, school, and community. The more focused and structured these early field experiences are, the more effective they can be in providing meaningful opportunities for learning. Because ethnographic research strategies are regarded as a superior means of identifying and learning about complex social environments (Bogdan & Biklen, 1998; Denzin, 1978), they offer a highly effective approach for focusing early field experiences. Students can use ethnographic research strategies to observe and participate in an early field experience, reflect on the practices they have observed, and gain an understanding of the social complexities of the observed environment (Diss & Kolenbrander, 1993).

A FIVE-STEP PROCESS

This model, developed by Ronald E. Diss over the past 12 years for Emory and Henry College in Virginia, uses a five-step process of ethnographic research techniques to provide structure and focus to early field experiences. Prior to their field experiences each semester, teacher education students receive 2 hours of instruction on how to conduct participant observations (Diss, 1990). They observe in classrooms a minimum of 16 hours per semester for a total of four semesters.

The students' observations are guided by no more than two questions they identify about a particular aspect of teaching and learning. They record descriptive field notes related to the two questions during or following all classroom observations.

Each semester, students also attend three 90-minute interactive seminars. These seminars provide opportunities for students to reflect upon their classroom observations with other students, professors, and practitioners. At the conclusion of each semester, students "pull together" what they have learned about the questions they examined by submitting a written analysis. In addition, an education professor interviews each student to discuss what was learned during the observations.

This early field experience model provides programmatic support and opportunities for teacher education students to acquire knowledge about both technical and reflective teaching skills. The five-step process is described in the following paragraphs.

STEP 1: Establishing purpose

At the end of each chapter of this text, there are suggestions for both school-based and community-based activities. The purpose of visiting schools and community-based social service agencies is to learn about the realities of schools, classrooms, and community agencies from a teaching or learning and family involvement perspective. This is accomplished by observing teachers and learners as they interact in real-life social situations. This is called "ethnography"—the study of people and their characteristics.

The purpose of ethnographic participant–observation strategies is to enable students to focus on teacher–student behaviors and characteristics during selected observations. Ethnographers pay attention to what the people observed say and do; how they say and do it; when, where, and with whom interactions occur; and what happens during and after interactions. When recording such information, students are collecting critical information about subtle yet salient features of classroom and community life that will enable them, over time, to identify patterns of behavior and relationships in given contexts. Prior to conducting observations, students should identify specific questions to focus their data collection.

STEP 2: Selecting questions

Classroom observations should begin with questions that reflect aspects of teaching. Examples of questions might be: What are effective ways to give directions to students? What are effective questioning techniques? How does the teacher avoid making some students feel left out during instruction? How does the teacher handle classroom management issues?

Community-based observations should begin with questions that provide insight into school, community, and family relationships. For example, students might investigate what types of resources are available to families in a particular school community. What, if any, financial assistance is available to families suffering from poverty? How do agencies offer counseling in parenting skills? What kind of relationship do the various community agencies have with teachers and administrators at the school?

Students may have an abundance of questions following their first early field experience. However, some "first-timers" may find it helpful to spend the first visit or two observing more generally, before selecting a particular question to investigate.

STEP 3: Conducting focused observations

With a specific question in mind, students will be able to conduct focused observations of classroom events related to that question. It is best to spend a minimum of 8 hours in the same environment focusing on their selected questions. By conducting repeated observations in the same environment, students will be able to see how frequently the contexts of social situations change. They will also be able to gather data about how teacher–student behavior may be related to these contextual changes.

As students focus observations on their questions, they should look for information related to the "nine dimensions" of social situations. These dimensions include space (the physical place), actors (the people involved), objects (physical things present), acts (single actions of actors), activities (set of related acts of actors), events (set of related activities actors carry out), time (sequencing that takes place over time), goals (things actors are trying to accomplish), and feelings (emotional behavior displayed by actors).

For example, if students are gathering information about a community cultural event as suggested at the end of Chapter 4 (e.g., a food fair, parade, or dance presentation), students should observe and record as much as they can about the social situation surrounding the event. What are the characteristics of the physical space in which the event takes place? Who are the leaders of the event? How do you know? What kind of interaction takes place between the leaders of the event and the audience? What are the goals of the event? Do people seem to be enjoying the event? How do you know? How do the people in attendance know what to do? Whom might you approach for information about the event?

During a 1-hour observation, there may be many events taking place (perhaps in rapid sequence). Students will not be able to record everything that happens. This will be especially true until they gain experience taking field notes. However, students will be surprised at the amount of significant descriptive data they will have gathered by the end of each observation.

STEP 4: Recording field notes

Field notes consist of any and all information collected related to the focal question, including observations, written material, publications, and clarifications by those observed. Field notes should include the date, time, and length of each observation.

Field notes will take the following forms:

- *Condensed notes* are fragmented notes, or "jottings" recorded as events unfold during classroom observations. These notes will serve as reminders to students when they expand their accounts later. Condensed notes should include only the essential details of the event being described.

  Because condensed notes are almost always written in haste, some students find it helpful to devise a system of shorthand, using T for *teacher*, S for *student*, and so forth to make note-taking easier. For example, this segment is taken from a student's condensed notes: T D,"bg I need u to lstn crflly." Lks w/ Ser fce, wats for sil, & attn of all. "Pls plce all fnshd wk in FB by 2." The segment is translated as: Teacher gives direction, "Boys and girls, I need you to listen carefully." She pauses, looks at the class with a serious face and waits for everyone to be silent and to focus on her, then continues, "Please place all finished work in the Finished Box by two o'clock."

If preservice teachers are participating (working directly with students) during classroom visitations, or interviewing staff members of a community agency, they will probably be unable to record condensed notes on the spot. When this happens, they should write notes immediately following visitations, recalling as many details as possible.

Condensed notes serve as reminders to students as they write expanded accounts following observations.

- *Expanded accounts* are a "filling out" of the condensed notes recorded earlier. Expanded accounts should describe behavior objectively; they should contain details of the events, including the setting, who did or said what to whom, what resulted, and so on. They should not include guesses of underlying motivations and subjective phrasing. For example, the comment "George's father was angry and in a fit of rage" makes an unwarranted assumption about George's father's feeling and motivation and is a statement that cannot be verified. "George's father turned red in the face, threw the papers on the floor, turned around abruptly, and walked out of the office slamming the door" describes behavior that can be verified. In general, be as precise and objective as possible without making assumptions about behavior. Avoid judgmental terms such as *nice, sad, happy,* and *angry.*

Expanded accounts will vary in length, but students generally produce three to five handwritten pages of text for every hour of observation. These accounts will serve as the basis for a two to three page formal report described in Step 5.

STEP 5: Constructing meaning through analysis and application

The fifth step in conducting ethnography is to analyze and interpret the data collected on the question studied. Students will reflect on these data to construct meaning about effective teaching or community–school relations. Their product will be a written report describing what they learned.

To analyze data, students should examine their expanded accounts for patterns of behavior and possible relationships between these behaviors and outcomes related to their question. Then they use this analysis to construct an "answer" to the question. For example, upon examining his expanded accounts, one student concluded that teachers have a good chance of having their instructions understood and followed when they insist on having the attention of every student before they communicate the instruction. Another student concluded that it is important when working with families to acknowledge the good things they are doing for their children.

Students' written responses will be a way of solidifying the application of their analysis of a situation. This "thinking on paper" will add to students' understanding of the knowledge and skills teachers and others need to interact effectively in complex environments. But, more important, students will have taken a big step in the process of acquiring a personal repertoire of ideas and beliefs about schools, communities, and families.

REFERENCES

Bogdan, R. C., & Biklen, S. K. (1998). *Qualitative research for education: An introduction to theory and methods* (3rd ed.) Boston : Allyn & Bacon.

Denzin, N. K. (1978). *The research act: A theoretical introduction to sociological methods.* New York: McGraw-Hill.

Diss, R. (1990). *Guidelines for classroom participation/observation using ethnographic strategies: A resource for conducting early field experiences.* Emory, VA: The Emory & Henry College Press.

Diss, R., & Thompson, E. (1994, February). Suggested procedures for conducting case study discussions. In Diane Foucar-Szocki (Ed.) *Case studies for teacher training and education leadership.* Harrisonburg, VA: Commonwealth Center for the Education of Teachers, James Madison University.

Diss, R. E., & Kolenbrander, R. W. (1993). What are teacher education students learning from early field experiences? *SRATE Journal, 2*(1), 34–39.

Appendix D

SUMMARY OF IDEA '97 REGULATORY ISSUES

In March 1999, after much controversy and many delays, the U.S. Department of Education published the federal regulations related to the 1997 reauthorization of IDEA, which is known as IDEA '97. (In the following section, Hallahan and Kauffman (2000) summarize some of the issues about which people frequently raise questions.)

IEPs AND THE GENERAL EDUCATION CURRICULUM IEPs must now include statements about how the student will not be involved in the general education classroom and curriculum.

INCLUSION IN STATE AND DISTRICT ASSESSMENTS Students with disabilities must now be included, with appropriate accommodations and modifications, in general assessments of educational progress mandated by the state or district.

INVOLVEMENT OF GENERAL EDUCATION TEACHERS At least one general education teacher must be involved in IEP development and informed of his or her responsibilities related to implementing the IEP.

GRADUATION AND DIPLOMAS The right to free, appropriate public education ends if the student graduates from high school with a regular diploma, but not if the student receives another type of diploma or certificate.

DISCIPLINE The school may remove a child for up to 10 school days at a time for any violation of school rules, as long as there is not a pattern of such removal. Students with disabilities can not be suspended long term or expelled for any behavior that is a manifestation of disability. Special education services must be continued for students with disabilities who are suspended (excepting the first 10 days of suspension in a school year) or expelled, regardless of whether the misbehavior is a manifestation of disability. If a student with disabilities has a weapon or drugs on school property or is substantially likely to injure others, then the school may move him or her to an interim alternative educational placement for up to 45 days.

FUNCTIONAL BEHAVIORAL ASSESSMENT AND POSITIVE BEHAVIORAL INTERVENTION PLANS If a student with disabilities is removed from school for more than 10 consecutive school days, then the IEP team must conduct a functional behavioral assessment and design a positive behavioral intervention plan to address the student's behavior.

CHARTER SCHOOLS IDEA and its regulations apply to all public agencies, including public charter schools.

Legislation is subject to change by Congress, regulations to change by administrative departments, both legislation and regulation to reinterpretation or to clarification by courts.

Source: Reprinted with permission of the publisher from Hallahan, D., & Kauffman, J. (2000). Exceptional Learners: Introduction to Special Education. *Boston: Allyn & Bacon.*

Index